Listen with Intention

How to Connect, Create Rapport, Develop Trust, and Build Deep Relationships

By: Devin White

ALL RIGHTS RESERVED

No part of this book may be reproduced, stored in a retrieval system, or transmitted in any form or by any means, electronic, mechanical, photocopying, recording, scanning, or otherwise, without the prior written permission of the publisher.

Limit of Liability/Disclaimer of Warranty: the publisher and the author make no representations or warranties with respect to the accuracy or completeness of the contents of this work and specifically disclaim all warranties, including without limitation warranties of fitness for a particular purpose. No warranty may be created or extended by sales or promotional materials. The advice and strategies contained herein may not be suitable for every situation. This work is sold with the understanding that the publisher is not engaged in rendering medical, legal or other professional advice or services. If professional assistance is required, the services of a competent professional person should be sought. Neither the publisher nor the author shall be liable for damages arising herefrom. The fact that an individual, organization or website is referred to in this work as a citation and/or potential source of further information does not mean that the author or the publisher endorses the information the individuals, organization or website may provide or recommendations they/it may make. Further, readers should be aware that websites listed on this work may have changed or disappeared between when this work was written and when it is read.

Table of Contents

Introduction 4

Chapter 1: What They Don't Tell You About Relationships 10

Chapter 2: Fundamentals of Listening 18

Chapter 3: Common Misconceptions 27

Chapter 4: Why Relationships Fall Apart 31

Chapter 5: Active Listening 41

Chapter 6: Five Levels of Communication and the Ego 47

Chapter 7: It All Starts with You 56

Chapter 8: Emotional Intelligence 62

Chapter 9: Getting Through to Others 76

Chapter 10: The Art of Connecting with Others 82

Chapter 11: Show Them You're Really Listening 88

Chapter 12: Persuasion or Empathy? 91

Chapter 13: Why Trust Matters 96

Chapter 14: Building a Deeper Connection 105

Chapter 15: Techniques for Listening with Intention 114

Chapter 16: How to Give People Space and Still Show That You Care 120

Chapter 17: Words That Build Trust in Any Relationship 123

Chapter 18: How to Read and Analyze People Better 129

Conclusion 138

Introduction

Relationships are at the heart of our human experience. Think about it—no matter where you go, what you do, or what your beliefs are, relationships influence your life. In both personal and business affairs, having a great relationship directly correlates with our level of happiness.

LinkedIn editors recently interviewed a well-known CEO of a Fortune 500 company to share his tips for leading a happy, successful life. One of the key ingredients he shared was finding a way to make the relationships in your life work. That includes your boss, colleagues, friends, family, and your love interests. You don't need to have many friends or be a people pleaser. Heck, you don't even need to agree with all your relatives, but learning the art of building trust, rapport, and the feeling that you care will go a long way in fueling your happiness tank as you go through life. At the core of any great human connection is the ability to listen to each other. You don't have control over whether others listen to you and "get you," but you can positively influence the interaction. That's what we're here to uncover.

As far back as I can recall, I struggled with this very topic, but I didn't realize it as such. As a kid in school, I had an okay time having a conversation with my friends (the few who got me) but struggled to have any meaningful discussion with most people. I ended up justifying it in my head that the majority of people were just weird. That there was something wrong with them.

Most people would speak, and I would start yawning. Whenever I tried to communicate something, it was like wax filled their ears. Nothing I said got through. The frustration of it all and my inexperience caused me to act in ways I am not too proud of, but I always pointed a finger and blamed it on the idiot who failed to understand me. It isn't that I hated people, and I was certainly no bully. I just hated that no one listened to me!

That went on right up to the time I landed my dream job. I worked so hard to get that position and was looking forward to working under some fantastic boss who would one day become my mentor, until I came face to face with "one of those people who didn't get me." This guy had no problem letting his employees know what he felt about their shortcomings. He thought they were all idiots. In my first staff meetings, I actually heard him use that phrase. No one dared protest. It seemed really odd to me that such a successful leader could treat people this way. After that first meeting, I started asking around if he was always like this, and it seemed unanimous. The boss was a world-class jerk, and people avoided one-on-one meetings with him at all costs. He was indeed a proficient executive, the best in the industry, yet he couldn't handle people?

Since I was the new kid at the office, it was easy for me to spot his wrong thinking. The boss didn't realize that he was always comparing other people to himself. His definition of idiocy was simply anyone who didn't act or think like him. He would call people names even I was guilty of using throughout my college years, like jackasses, rude bastards, and so on. Now, I had never gotten as far as calling anyone an idiot (at least not to their face) but nonetheless, having this experience with my boss awoke me to a painful truth: If I didn't change something about myself and how I interacted with and handled people, I would have a very miserable professional and social life. So, I did something brave. I reflected on myself in the mirror one weekend and asked some painful questions. Questions like, why is it that I still have no real social life? And how is it that every person I date always has too many flaws for something real to develop? Why do people constantly interrupt me when speaking as though they have no respect for my ideas?

Lying down in bed on a Saturday night, feeling rather hopeless and wondering what it would take for me to be in an enriching relationship, I decided to do something drastic. The thought of ending up like my boss was appalling to me and enough motivation to seek out transformation in how I communicated.

I swapped binge-watching romance movies and began binge-reading and binge-watching anything and everything I could find on relationships and the psychology behind effective communication.

I scoured the Internet for renowned experts who taught on this topic and found myself falling deeper and deeper into a rabbit hole. Don't worry. This book will not bore you with psychological jargon and terms that add no meaning to your current quest. Instead, I have condensed years of expert research, my own experiments, and discovered hacks that have put me at the top of my game when it comes to relationships. I no longer wallow in self-pity as my life is rich with excellent relationships both professionally and personally. My new marriage has never felt stronger, and I can indeed attest to the fact that my happiness tank is full and steady thanks to the work I did. The blueprint of how I turned my life and relationships around is laid out for you in bite-sized chapters. All you need to do is commit to reading all the way to the end, implement the simple exercises when presented to you, and just trust in this process.

My promise to you is that by the time you're through with this book, you'll be able to establish a genuine connection with whomever you choose, whether in a professional or casual setting. You'll also learn the art of building deep personal relationships with your loved ones and the science of rapport.

Why Learn How to Listen and Build Relationships?

Reason #1: The first and foremost reason you should prioritize and train yourself to listen with intention and build rapport is to gain a skill set you can use for the rest of your life. That skill set will help you in personal and professional relationships.

Reason #2: Learning how to actively listen also enables you to increase self-awareness. As you'll get to learn shortly, your ability to listen and get through to others depends on how present and mindful you are. Now, why would self-awareness even matter when it comes to building relationships? That brings me to my next point.

Reason #3: Mindfulness and being present makes it easy for you to practice empathy. When you are present in-the-moment, you can understand the other person's feelings, and you can read between the lines and figure out the best way to communicate with them.

Reason #4: You'll do a better job at interviews or whenever you're speaking with decision-makers and key people who can sway circumstances in your favor. Think for a moment of a time when you needed to say something to a client, prospect, or a loved one, but you were shooting blanks. Imagine if you had the techniques and this skill of being able to convince that person. I think things would have gone much smoother in just a matter of minutes, am I right?

How This Skill Will Protect You and Help You Succeed More in Your Professional Career

The better you get at listening with intention, the easier it will be to help other people understand you. How? Because you will have the ability to create a secure arena for communication where they can communicate on your terms.

If you didn't realize it yet, everyone communicates on their own terms. They filter everything through their beliefs, frames of reference, and preconceived ideas. The better you get at this, the more powerful you become because you can focus your energy on understanding rather than reacting, either consciously or unconsciously, as you interact with others.

This is something we all need. There's a certain level of flexibility we need to develop so we can vary our style of communication, mostly when we speak with people who are different from us. The truth is, no matter how eloquent you are as an individual or how acceptable your style of communication, you will always find people around you who function differently; people who don't "get you," and you can't just base your method of communicating on your own preferences. That will lead to a very limited life.

So, what you need is a simple approach to building rapport in a genuine way that leverages your strengths and amplifies your ability to communicate with others. This book doesn't make grand claims of making you the best communicator in the world. No book can do that. But you will have a sound working knowledge of how to improve yourself and, in turn, impact your interactions. If that is something you value, then the following chapters hold the key to a brand-new experience of relationships in your world. Let's get started.

Chapter 1: What They Don't Tell You About Relationships

"You can't not communicate. Everything you say and do or don't say and don't do sends a message to others." — *John Woods*

Here's a question that you've probably asked with no satisfying answer: Why is it that some people never stop talking while others can barely get a word out? And how is it that some people continuously interrupt others during a conversation while others seem to be total blockheads, always missing the point being made? And while we are on this topic, have you ever been in a situation where you're talking to a person, and as soon as you finish, they respond with something completely unrelated to what you just said—which makes you wonder if they were even listening at all?

Yeah. Relationships can be challenging. It can feel like an uphill climb, especially when dealing with people who don't think and act like you, which will be the majority of the people you encounter in your lifetime. And this doesn't apply to work relationships only. It could even be with the person you end up marrying. No two people are precisely the same. But it is crucial to understand how to handle all kinds of people because that is the key to a happy, successful life. That's why I see this as more of a quest.

I know you want to start influencing and building rapport with others, but you're going to have to do something brave in order to do that. You'll need to look in the mirror and begin with transforming that person. Whether you realize it or not, the great secret to successful relationships and effective communication is understanding yourself. The more you can understand yourself and develop certain qualities, the easier it will be to have the kind of connections you desire.

The Starting Point

No one is born a master communicator. Communicating is a skill that we all learn as we grow. So don't worry if you're not as great as the guys giving TED Talks. You may not be as eloquent as an orator or as brilliant as a New York Times bestselling author, but I can assure you, none of these individuals became what they are by chance or accident. They've worked on developing this life skill, and with a bit of effort on your part, you can at least become good enough to influence the relationships that matter to you.

The main thing to remember is that communication is a two-way process. We continuously switch roles over and over in the process of rapport and trust-building. In one phase, we are sending information, and in the next, we are receiving information. To be an effective communicator, you will need to learn how to be on either side of the table. Not only do you need to improve your speaking skills, but you'll need to brush up on being a great listener.

A Relationship is a Dialogue, not a Monologue.

I played a lot of tennis with my dad while growing up. Though I'm not very athletic, I enjoyed that sport. One of the things I realized is that it helped me become better coordinated and trained me to pay attention to the person on the other end serving the ball. I use this as an analogy for how relationships work.

Relationships are a two-way street. They require a back-and-forth movement where both parties feel respected, valued, and a part of the game. It involves exchanging energy and information held together by a foundation of respect that cannot be counterfeit. So to have a successful dialogue, you need to become a good listener.

Have you ever wondered why we have two ears and one mouth? It's because we need to exercise twice as much listening as speaking for a successful conversation to take place. And here we fall into the main challenge of developing strong relationships: how to be a great listener.

That will be our main focus throughout this book. You will learn techniques that will help you demonstrate and practice the art of listening and tips on how to build trust and rapport quickly. As you do, you'll find yourself fast becoming proficient at handling all kinds of people regardless of their temperament and communication style. Think of it like riding a bike. First, you need to get on the bike, and then and only then can you figure out what you need to do.

How Humans Communicate

If you want to build rapport and develop deeper connections, you'll need to learn a thing or two about how humans communicate. We don't just communicate through words. In fact, there are four main ways we communicate with each other: verbally, nonverbally, visually, and through written words. Let's briefly look at each of these pathways.

- Verbal communication is the use of language and the most common way to engage with others. It is efficient and can be used under almost every circumstance but to do it right, you need to use active listening skills and speak with confidence. It would help if you also became aware of your tone of voice to avoid passing on the wrong message.

- Nonverbal is the use of body language, facial expressions, and gestures to convey information. Most of the time, we use it unintentionally, especially if we aren't aware of our body movement as we engage with another. This unconscious exchange can easily lead to conflicting messages, especially when what you're speaking is different from what your body says. That would throw off the receiving party and, more often than not, break any chance of rapport. For example, have you ever bumped into a friend who said: "I am doing well," yet something in you felt "off" as though she wasn't telling the truth? Sure, she was smiling, but you just didn't buy it. That might be because your friend's body language contradicted what she said, and your subconscious picked up on it. The importance of understanding your body language cannot be overemphasized because trust-building, which we'll talk about later, relies heavily on the alignment of your body language and active listening.

- Written communication is the act of writing, typing, or printing symbols like letters and numbers to convey information. It's simple and usually doesn't rely on tone of voice as much as the first two.

- Visual form of communication includes using imagery and things like photographs, drawings, charts, emojis, and such to convey information. In the era of social media and apps like WhatsApp and Instagram, paying more attention to the imagery you use when communicating with friends, colleagues, and associates has become vital. It's essential to consider the receiver, your relationship with that person, and the meaning your visual imagery will convey before using any pictures and emojis. The right imagery under the wrong context can create conflict, and the right one under the right conditions can deepen a connection with someone. That's why you should consider this even as you learn the art of active listening.

Body Language

A large percentage of communication is taken up by body language. If you want to build rapport with someone and develop trust, understanding your body language and using it to communicate the right message will go a long way in making you a master communicator. It will also give you an edge when it comes to reading people.

So, what is body language? It includes posture, movements, intonation, pitch, and facial expressions. For example, we can all tell when someone gives a genuine smile from their eyes, not just the mouth and teeth. How a person moves different parts of their body can tell us a lot and often conveys a particular thought or feeling that our minds seem to interpret quickly. Body language appears to be a universal form of communication, although culture may create some variations. Here's a quick overview of what you need to pay attention to regarding your body posture and movement.

Eye contact:
When speaking with someone, do your best to maintain eye contact—without coming across as creepy, of course. Avoid having shifty eyes as that makes you seem like you're disinterested or as though you have something to hide.

Posture:
A steady, upright posture will convey confidence as you engage with someone, and people tend to trust someone who speaks with confidence and authority. Watch your spinal alignment so that you still convey an upright appearance without coming across as stiff if you're sitting or standing. If you're sitting across from someone, you can lean slightly toward them as that expresses interest and engagement. Also, remember to keep your arms in a position that sends a warm and open signal. Crossed arms should be avoided as much as possible, especially if you're trying to build rapport with someone new.

Hand gestures and movement:
Most people have no idea what to do with their hands when engaged in a conversation. Here's what you shouldn't be doing

if you want someone to perceive you as authoritative. Don't fiddle with your fingers, play with your hair, or twirl your thumbs. Excessive hand movements suggest nervousness. If you're standing, avoid keeping your hands in your pocket as this sends a negative subconscious signal to the other person. People always feel better when they can see your hands. You can do a few things with your hands to indicate self-confidence, including resting your hands gently by your side if standing or on your lap if sitting. When meeting someone for the first time, use a firm handshake and make eye contact simultaneously.

Mirroring:
The mirror technique is recommended by many experts and involves reflecting the same emotions the other person conveys. You can also mirror their body movement but be subtle about it because timing is everything. By giving the same nonverbal cues as nodding and smiling as you listen, the other person feels like you are listening and that you care. If you're engaged in a serious topic, mirror that same distress in your expression.

Most men struggle with this, which is why small arguments pop up when a woman brings up a topic she cares about. Often she will feel as though the man doesn't listen or care about her frustration. All that can be easily avoided if you just mirror the emotions she is conveying.

Smile:
This is one of the best-kept secrets if you want to develop deeper connections with people. A genuine smile at your spouse, partner, colleague, or anyone else can help them feel

relaxed and understood. Let me emphasize that this must be a genuine smile, not flattery or a fake smile that doesn't activate most of your facial muscles. People are good at detecting that.

When you smile, show a little of your teeth, crinkle your eyes a little, and let your smile fade slowly.

Chapter 2: Fundamentals of Listening

"Listening is an art that requires attention over talent, spirit over ego, others over self." — Dean Jackson

By now, you should realize that becoming a master communicator and developing trust begins with a desire to understand. Before others can understand you, you must seek to understand others. The more you know yourself and your personality, the easier it is to understand others, which naturally develops the empathy needed to communicate effectively.

Why You Need to Think Before You Speak

You can never really become a master at building rapport if you don't develop the habit of thinking before spilling out your words. Realize that words are powerful, and if you want to become an influencer and someone people trust, you need to make every word count. The more you think about carefully choosing your words, the more value people will give to those words, causing them to pay attention. Consider Nelson Mandela or Obama. Regardless of your political views on these men, they are equally powerful when it comes to effective communication. Whenever Nelson Mandela would speak, people always listened. It isn't just because he carried himself the right way and used the right body language. It's also because he is a man who always chose his words carefully. Watch a video clip on YouTube if you haven't seen any of his famous speeches.

Words define our identity and reveal our attitudes and sensitivities. They reflect who we are. So, our word choice will show the listener how intelligent or ignorant we are, and the more we speak, the more that impression gets reinforced. A great exercise is to develop the habit of thinking before talking to someone. How do you do this?

There are several ways in which you can plan your speech. In fact, psycholinguistic research shows that we do plan our speech in different ways and that we do think in advance to various degrees. Hence, if it is a planned speech, be thorough with your word choice and each sentence's meaning. If it's a casual interaction, listen and comprehend before opening your mouth. Develop that buffer period so you can hold your tongue and avoid throwing up the first thought that enters your head.

Techniques to Help You Think Before You Speak

One great technique you can utilize is pressing your internal pause button. Did you know you have the ability to mentally say "pause" as though you have a remote control, and nothing will come out of your mouth? By hitting that internal pause, you can process the information you just received and your ongoing thoughts to give an assessment of how to proceed. And if you take a few deep breaths while on this pause, you can bring oxygen to your brain, which assists with planning your speech. Once you feel calm and right enough to say what you want to say, mentally press "play."

Another technique you can apply is going through the following questions quickly and assessing your words before speaking them aloud:
Is it **T**rue?
Is it **H**elpful?
Is it **I**nspiring?
Is it **N**ecessary?
Is it **K**ind?

If what you're about to say doesn't pass the thinking test, hold your tongue and keep listening.

Words have the power to build or destroy relationships, they can move people into action, and they can create a perception of authority and respect only when you, as the speaker, have developed this habit. A good rule of thumb which you can start testing is to wait five to ten seconds before responding to someone to give your brain time to apply one of the techniques you just learned. Don't worry about that time lag. It's not as awkward as you think, and people will prefer that you take your time rather than spill out words that you'll wish you could take back.

Five Fundamentals for Effective Listening

#1: Attending to Nonverbal Behaviors
In the last chapter, you learned about body language and the important role it plays in building rapport and gaining trust. Your body cues will alert the person speaking or listening to

you in negative or positive ways. If you have practiced the suggestions made earlier, then you're more aware of your body and the signals you're sending out when engaged in conversation. The key is to ensure you send out desired signals. You don't want to be sending off signals that you'd rather be elsewhere or that you're nervous. When someone speaks to you, are you smiling and nodding along as they share in their excitement? Are you projecting a condescending or disapproving look as they share their ideas? Are you leaning toward them as you speak or leaning back with your arms folded? When someone speaks to you, your body language should communicate, "go ahead, I'm listening, and I care about your opinion." When you talk, your body should say, "I'm confident, trustworthy, I care, and I value your attention."

#2: Asking Questions

Asking questions is a great way to build rapport. But not all questions are created equal, and you need to identify the best questions to match particular situations. For example, if you're trying to dive deeper and develop a connection with someone, ask open-ended questions. If you want to invoke reflection in another, ask prompting questions. Use closed-ended questions when you want to limit the conversation and find out specific information.

#3: Reflecting Feelings

This is the art of capturing someone's feelings and restating them in a nonjudgmental way. It demonstrates to the person that you're engaged, and that you're aware of the emotion the other person is attempting to share. Examples include using phrases such as "it sounds like you're really..." (angry, disappointed, hurt, etc.) or "I can sense your ..." (frustration, sadness, anxiety, etc.). The other person feels like you get them by expressing this, which makes them trust you more.

#4: Paraphrasing

Paraphrasing shows that you heard what was said. It is handy when you are the one listening. It's a key component of active listening because the speaker feels like you understood what was being shared. Paraphrasing basics include restating keywords or specific phrases that the speaker used in the same sequence they were spoken. When doing this, try not to sound like a robot or copycat. Make it natural.

#5: Summarizing

This is the skill of concisely recapping what the speaker said over a longer period of time. You don't need to capture exactly what they said, but you need to convey the ideas, feelings, and action items that the speaker shared. Some people take notes to follow the order and sequence of information conveyed. That can be an excellent tip to implement when it's a formal interaction. For social conversations, you just need to share the gist and any critical information.

Five Levels of Listening

Did you know that we listen at different levels? It's not enough to be present. It would be best if you also practiced active listening. We'll dive deeper into what active listening is all about but before that, let's address the five levels that we and everyone else listens at. The level at which one listens determines how much they get out of an interaction.

#1: Level One – Ignoring

This is the lowest level of listening. It basically means the person isn't listening to a word you say. They are probably distracted by something or caught up in their own inner dialogue. How can you tell someone isn't listening to you?

Notice their body language. What signals are they sending? Perhaps they are on their phone as you speak? Another thing that might give them away is the fact that they might interject with a topic that has nothing to do with what you've been talking about. In all these cases, you can be sure the person hasn't paid attention to you, and you'll need to take a different approach if you desire to convey your message to them.

#2: Level Two – Pretend Listening

Have you ever been engaged in a conversation with someone who looks like they are a million miles away? You could even say a ridiculous thing and they would nod in agreement. In other words, this is someone who is trying hard to pretend that they are listening to you, but they are distracted, and if you observe their body language, you can tell they aren't engaged in your topic. Over the phone, it's pretty common whereby a person is talking to you while browsing on their laptop or checking emails.

#3: Level Three – Selective Listening

At this level, the person is partially listening to you. They might only pay attention to things that they feel interested in or agree with, but as soon as you start talking about something they don't care about, they switch to pretend listening. If they are ill-mannered, they might even drop to level one and completely tune you out.

#4: Level Four – Attentive Listening

Attentive listening is the fourth level. It's where the other person is, in fact, carefully listening to you but carrying on a debate in their head about whether they agree or disagree with you. They are finding the right and wrong in your words. So instead of listening, they are formulating a response based on their prejudice and biases.

#5: Level Five – Empathic Listening

This is the level we want to get your listeners to. At this level, someone is paying attention to you with empathy, meaning they feel, identify with, and understand what you're saying. When others listen to you at this level, your words create an impact, and developing trust becomes easy and natural. The same is true when you listen to others at this level. Empathy shouldn't be confused with sympathy. Sympathy is feeling sorry for someone, whereas empathy is feeling what the other feels.

How to Get Others to Listen to You from Level Five

If you want to get people to get you and have empathic listening, it will have to start with you. After going through the five levels, can you only identify the level you predominantly operate when others speak to you? Perhaps you keep shifting from one level to another, but there's going to be one that's more dominant than the rest.

The goal here isn't to judge or shame yourself. Instead, you want to bring awareness to your current level of listening aptitude so you can move toward empathic listening. The better you become at empathic listening, the easier it will be for others to reciprocate.

A few things you can do to practice empathic listening are:
1. Learn to listen to the speaker without interrupting them.
2. Show a genuine interest in what's being said. Do your best to understand what the person is saying. You can even ask questions to get clarification and to ensure you're following their train of thought.
3. Avoid entertaining that inner dialogue while someone speaks to you. Thinking about what you're going to say to someone while they talk makes you a poor listener.
4. Don't judge, condemn, or resent what the other person says even if you disagree. Have an open mind and allow everyone to have their opinion. That will create a sense of psychological safety which everyone likes to have as they express their opinion.

You can also apply the four stages of empathic listening into your framework.

Stage 1: Mirror what is being said. Repeat the last few words that you heard in order to get further understanding.

Stage 2: Say what you hear without adding anything new, especially when you want clarification.

Stage 3: Reflect on the feeling being conveyed. Try to grasp the sentiment the other person is expressing. Go beyond mere words and try to connect with the meaning.

Stage 4: Restate what was said as you connect with the feeling. This helps you understand the full context and meaning of the message being conveyed.

I know what you're thinking. This sounds like a lot of work. And you're right. It does take some effort, especially in the beginning, but the payoff is well worth it.

Chapter 3: Common Misconceptions

"We have but two ears and one mouth so that we may listen twice as much as we speak." — *Thomas Edison*

Before you can truly begin to master effective communication skills, you need to shake up some of the long-held beliefs that often damage your ability to achieve what you want. Here are the main ones that tend to hinder effective communication.

#1: Effective communication is about speaking bluntly

You'll find many people, and maybe you've even said this yourself, who believe "I tell it how it is, and if people can't deal with reality, that's their problem." Unfortunately, that will only get in the way of influencing and getting through to others. Truth divorced from empathy can be very hurtful and hinder your ability to build trust and rapport. I'm not advocating that you lie or give people erroneous information or false praise just to avoid conflict. Lies are unnecessary. It's very possible to be known as someone who speaks the truth even when it's harsh or painful and still be highly respected. The key is to develop compassion. The more you build your emotional intelligence, the easier it will be for you to speak with kindness and truth at all times.

#2: Communication is a monologue

In this day of technology, there's a lot of broadcasting and one-way communication that many of us have been exposed to. Radios, televisions, and social media are often used to broadcast a message, not genuinely communicate something meaningful. It seems our relationships are starting to fall victim to this state. Look at your last WhatsApp or text chats and notice how you have been framing your conversations. Does it really encourage dialogue? Is it just a monologue? For most people, their ability to develop trust and communication is tied to this common misconception.

#3: Over 90% of all communication is nonverbal

There's a widespread myth that body language or nonverbal communication constitutes most of the communication. That's not accurate.

Here's the truth about this myth. Albert Mehrabian, Professor Emeritus of Psychology at the University of California in Los Angeles, and Susan Ferris looked at the contribution of verbal and nonverbal signals to total communication in a study titled "Inference of Attitudes from Nonverbal Communication in Two Channels." The two researchers had participants listen to pre-recorded voices of single words such as "maybe" while looking at black and white photographs of facial expressions. Participants were told the tonality of voices and facial expressions communicated disliking, liking, or neutrality. They were then asked to choose between the three attitudes for each recording. The study found facial expressions contribute 55% while vocalists contribute 38% to communication. It's a 3:2 ratio. Mehrabian later wrote a book, *Silent Messages: Implicit Communication of Emotions and Attitudes*, in which he also defined a rule based on his earlier study. The rule suggests that 7% of meaning is in the spoken words, 38% of meaning is in how we say the words, and 55% of meaning is in body language. Mehrabian explicitly states that 93% of nonverbal contribution to communication applies only when someone discusses his or her dislikes and likes. Again, this cannot be used as a general rule for communication because unless you are speaking about personal preferences and prejudices, body language may not be the only thing to consider.

#4: Intellectual intelligence equals excellent communication

Having a high IQ doesn't automatically make you a great communicator. It doesn't naturally cause people to want to listen to you. In fact, in TV shows, the most intelligent person in the room is often portrayed as snobbish and arrogant. It's not uncommon to see people making fun of such individuals, especially if they also come across as boring.

We also see teenagers completely ignoring their parents, not because they consider their guardians dumb but because they lack a connection with what's being said. A person with a high IQ might struggle to get their message across primarily because they lack emotional intelligence, which is key to building a connection with someone. So, if you've been wondering why no one pays attention to your talks or buys into your brilliant ideas, it might be time to assess your emotional intelligence as that weighs in far more than your IQ.

#5: Successful communication is when you come away feeling good

Many people assume they have succeeded at building rapport when they come away feeling good after speaking with logic, telling the truth, and demonstrating how intelligent they are. This is far from the truth. George Bernard Shaw, a Nobel Prize winner for Literature, said, "The single biggest problem in communication is the illusion that it has taken place."

Good communication, therefore, isn't about what you do but instead, it's about creating an atmosphere where openly understanding a genuine exchange takes place. The person listening to you needs to walk away feeling better than they did before speaking with you. They need to feel like they were part of something. So that means their response should be the indicator of how effective you are as a communicator.

Chapter 4: Why Relationships Fall Apart

"In a relationship, when communication starts to fade, everything else follows." — Unknown

Do you know why most relationships fall apart? It usually comes down to a handful of things, including the fact that you're not a good listener, perhaps you don't speak your truth clearly, there's no trust between the two of you, or you're not present enough with the other person. The bottom line is that regardless of the circumstantial evidence, relationships ultimately crumble when the individuals involved don't take full responsibility for how they show up in that relationship. This applies to both professional and personal relations. So, the first thing we need to do is clarify the significant role effective communication and trust-building will have in your relationships. Communication and trust go hand in hand. Miss one and your relationship is likely to fail.

When it comes to communication, you need to master both your verbal and nonverbal communication to avoid sending contradictory signals. If you want to use communication to develop trust and build rapport, you're going to have to get comfortable with sharing your feelings as well as your thoughts.

Imagine you're talking to yourself when communicating with others.

The golden rule "treat others as you would like to be treated" applies to your effectiveness as a communicator. Now, there's no guarantee that you will always receive the same benefits you give others, but it's still the right thing to do. It's a lot easier to become a respected leader when others feel like you respect them. And it's also a lot easier to have people pay attention and actively listen to you when you demonstrate active listening while engaged with others. The words you use, the tone, and the manner in which you relate to others should be acceptable to your own ego. In other words, before you label someone as something or call them a specific name or describe them in a particular way, either to their face or behind their backs, do a "check-in" to see how you would feel if the tables were turned and the same was happening to you. If it feels right for you, then proceed in complete confidence that you are true to yourself. You can also use the "THINK" technique.

Communication in an Intimate Relationship

Intimate relationships are often more complicated than regular relationships. Things get more problematic when one is a poor communicator or struggles to develop trust. And some of the things that stand in the way of proper communication with a loved one include too much stress or pressure, a lack of focus, inconsistent body language, or broken trust. To start repairing an existing relationship, here are some steps you can take:

Step #1: Become more engaged and active as you listen

Instead of focusing on the right thing to say in response to your loved one, focus on understanding the information being conveyed. Tap into their emotions and see if you can feel where they are. There's a big difference between being a passive and an active listener. By focusing on understanding the other person and their point of view, they feel heard and respected, which will help you develop a stronger connection.

Try to set aside your tendency to judge or interrupt the speaker during an intimate conversation. When it's your turn to speak, be mindful of your tone, the response you give, and your body language, especially your facial expression.

Step #2: Keep a lid on your stress levels

Have you ever had a stressful day only to have things get worse due to a disagreement with a loved one that caused you to explode on their trivial argument? When we are stressed, communication is more challenging because our emotions tend to inhibit our reasoning faculty. And if you happen to talk to a loved one who also had a stressful day, things can get out of hand pretty fast. Imagine a scenario where a husband arrives home after a long pressure-filled day, culminating in a deal that went south thanks to a teammate who screwed up. He walks in and finds his wife sulking in the kitchen. As he tries to reach for a kiss, she brushes him off and yells, "Why do you always forget to take out the trash when it's your turn? It's as though you never want to help around here!" Chances of that turning into a full-blown argument where both parties end up saying something they'll regret are high—all because this couple did not adequately manage emotions and stress levels.

To avoid similar situations, I encourage you to use stalling tactics that will enable you to have some time to cool down.

Use the pause technique to collect your thoughts and dial down the emotional charge of negativity. Deliver your words clearly and maintain a calm tone of voice once you choose to respond, and whatever you do, please do not engage your loved one in a pointless blame game.

Whenever you notice your body getting stressed, e.g., tensed muscles, tightening stomach, fist-clenching, heart rate, and temperature increase, take a moment to calm down before deciding to continue that conversation.

What to Do if the Other Person Isn't Listening to a Word You Say

Sometimes, no matter how much we try, the other person isn't stable enough emotionally to listen to us. In such cases, we have a few options. We can attempt to calm their emotions and mind before repeating ourselves, we can pause in silence to recapture their attention, or we can step away from that environment and create some distance for a time. If you're in a room, consider leaving the room or going to the terrace for a little while. Take a pause before conveying your message again. Then come back to it when the air is cool once more, and everyone can listen with a calm head.

How You Speak and What You Say Are Equally Important

You might think that all you have to do is say the right words and you immediately get the desired results. That would be an erroneous judgment on your part. Consider the words "I love you." Three different guys can speak these three words to the same woman, and she will have completely different reactions. To one guy, she might giggle and reply, "me too," giving him a light brotherly hug because he is, in fact, her brother. Guy number two might get smacked in the face or get red wine poured all over his white shirt as she rebukes him in disgust and calls him a pervert and the third guy, well, he may just end up marrying the girl as she passionately responds, "I love you more." In all these scenarios, the exact three words were said, but how they were spoken made all the difference.

It turns out, being a great speaker isn't just about saying the right words. It's also about the tone of voice, pitch, volume, pace, facial expression, and context.

A recent study by psychology researcher Jose Benki at the U-M Institute for Social Research (ISR) used recordings of over 1380 introductory phone calls to see what variables in people's speech correlated with their success in convincing people to participate in a survey—in other words, communicating effectively to reach the desired result. They found that the above-mentioned speech cues played a significant role in whether a person accepted or declined. The take-home point for you is that you need to learn your speech cues and figure out how to improve them. Do you need to speed up or slow down? Do you use the right tone and pitch when delivering important messages? Do you say the right words in the right way at the right time?

Preventing or Avoiding Poor Communication and Arguments in Your Relationship

Many psychologists have been studying communication for a long time, and there are several communication models that experts recommend we experiment with, especially if we wish to avoid quarrels. Among them is the "Four Ears," or the four-sided model developed by Friedemann Schulz von Thun (1981). This theory states that every message contains four different pieces of information. These are Fact (what I inform, which includes statements, facts, and data), Self-revealing (what I reveal about myself as the speaker), Relationship (what I think about you and how we get along), and Appeal (what I want to make you do/how I want to influence you). More often than not, we only verbally convey one piece of that four-piece model, but the rest still get passed on subconsciously as the other person listens to you. Based on the other person's filter, beliefs, and perceptions, they react in the desired way or turn in the opposite direction.

For example, you say to a loved one, "The trash hasn't been taken out." The other person won't care so much about that fact but what they feel it implies. Perhaps they interpret the tone as you being pushy, calling them lazy, unreliable, and unhelpful around the house, which leads to an outburst on their end. Instead of taking out the trash, they yell and storm out of the house, and you're left thinking, "What the heck just happened?"

Biased expectations and attitudes, personal history, fears, and concerns can lead to miscommunication and misunderstandings. So, what is the secret to avoiding these fallouts? Metacommunication. A big part of that involves active listening, which we'll discuss at length in the next chapter. You also need to be willing to approach and perceive issues in a nonjudgmental way. This can be a great technique to use when you're trying to change or influence some action. Follow these four steps:

1. Observe facts without interpreting or evaluating the meaning.

You want to get into the habit of observing without judging or labeling someone or something as bad or wrong. If a friend, loved one, or employee comes late to your meeting, recognize that the fact is they were late, nothing more. It's not a sign of disinterest or disrespect. Avoid reading too much into it. So instead of buying into your interpretation of what this could mean, you could simply say, "I realize you are late for our meeting/date." That is a factual observation without any evaluation.

2. Communicate feelings and thoughts.

Secondly, it is vital that you communicate your feelings instead of hiding or suppressing them. Arguments usually arise when feelings have been repressed. Speak your emotions with as much empathy and compassion as you can manage. If you're genuinely annoyed about the fact that the person is late, let them know. Speak your mind. You could say, "I'm curious and a little bothered by your lateness as it makes me wonder whether you value this meeting/date."

3. Express what you need.

Let the other person clearly understand what you need. If you care about being treated in a particular way, express this need. You could say, "I'd like to be treated with consideration."

4. Make a clear request.

The last step you can take to ensure the other person understands you is to make your request explicitly known. Ensure that you get confirmation from the other person that they understand what you mean as you speak. Going back to the same example, you could say, "What I am requesting is that you do your best to arrive at our agreed upon time in the future. Is that okay?" As you get a nod or verbal consent back, you can be confident that the listener received your communication.

Equally as important as speaking clearly, and becoming a great listener, you also need to learn how to respond constructively to the feedback others give you. We will also touch on this as the book unfolds, but a good rule of thumb is to embrace the other person's opinion and get curious about why they say what they say. Whether you agree with someone's feedback or not, you can still receive their input and allow them the same respect of communicating their thoughts.

How to Say and Do the Right Thing at the Right Time

If you want to ensure that you say the right thing most of the time, you will need to develop the ability to identify "context" as fast as possible. When it's a close friend, family member, or spouse, this might not be too hard, but you should also develop this sensitivity to colleagues, employees, and even strangers. Realize that the person you're speaking to has trigger words and words that cause them to appreciate and listen to you more attentively. If you can figure out what resonates with them better and reach for those words, you're more likely to get the desired outcome.

It's not always easy to know what to say or when to say what you want, but there are certain words that we know hinder healthy communication and others that promote it better. If you know what some of these things are, use them to your advantage. Let's start with a few phrases to avoid:

What's wrong with you?
Why are you getting so upset?
That's not my problem.

Here are some constructive phrases that promote healthy communication:

I'm listening.
I understand.
How are you feeling?
I see where you're coming from.
Help me understand your point of view.

Tips on How to Say and Do the Right Thing

• Be thoughtful of the words you're about to speak and make sure they elicit the desired response.

- Before speaking, imagine you are the person you're speaking to.

- As you convey your emotions, be mindful of your body language and your emotions. Do your best to keep your emotions in check.

- Be gentle and empathetic as you deliver tough, painful, or sad information.

- Get into the habit of giving an encouraging word to everyone you speak with. Find something you can praise, celebrate, or compliment them on. Notice how powerful this simple exercise is in developing deeper connections.

- Discipline your thoughts and create a buffer period so you can think through what you want to say. Keep yourself in check, and don't let your ego get in the way. That will ensure you hold the right space for exchange (the very essence of communication).

Chapter 5: Active Listening

"Listening is an act of love. When you listen to people, you are communicating nonverbally that they are important to you."
— *Jim George*

Let's test your listening skills. Think for a moment about the last five conversations you've had. What were you doing when the other person was speaking? Were you texting, eating, or thinking about an upcoming meeting? Most of us are accustomed to what's referred to as passive listening. That's what I just described above.

This chapter is going to show you another approach to listening referred to as active listening. Active listening is the key to developing trust and a connection, and it involves you being 100% present and focused on the person speaking to you. Active listening involves all your senses, not just the ears, and it also engages your emotions. I like to think of it as listening with your ears and heart.

Signs that you are an active listener include how you use your body (posture, facial expression, etc.) and how good you are at reflecting or mirroring the other person's feelings.

When people feel like you are present with them and that you "get them," they are more likely to trust and confide in you. They will also listen in return and will see you as someone with authority in their lives.

Developing a Discerning Ear

If you want to activate your ability to listen genuinely, here are some things you can do to train your ear to do more than just hear.

#1: Be silent and attentive until the other person is done speaking

Sometimes we are already working on a reply before the speaker is finished talking. That increases the chances of miscommunication, and it almost always triggers a negative emotion in the speaker as they realize you weren't really paying attention. So, you need to pause and allow those few magical seconds of silence to pass before jumping in with your response. That does two things: it shows the speaker you were paying full attention and that you got the entire message. You also get that much-needed buffer time to process the information that the speaker gave to you.

#2: Reflect on what you heard

The inner chatter that usually goes on in our heads can inhibit our ability to grasp the information being conveyed fully. So, I want you to get into the habit of repeating back what the speaker said. That will help the person know if you're on the same page or not. If the speaker needs to reword their statement until you understand, that's perfectly normal. It's this back-and-forth exchange that ensures a successful dialogue occurs.

#3: Start listening to learn and understand

Instead of just listening to someone out of courtesy or politeness, start listening to people because you're genuinely curious about the other person's viewpoint. Authentic communication involves dialogue. If you want people to act on your words, you need to become interested in understanding others and respecting their views even when they differ from yours.

How to Actively Listen with Empathy

- Become aware of the speaker's body language but don't get distracted by it

While it is nice to be mindful of your speaker's body, face, and overall demeanor, I don't recommend reading too much into it. You might soon find yourself wandering and absent from the actual conversation. Read the context and keep in mind that your main emphasis should be remaining present and engaged in the words being spoken.

- Try to match the rhythm of your breathing to the rhythm of the speaker's breathing

Studies have shown that when people breathe at the same rate, it creates a resonance that makes it easier to move at similar paces and speak on similar pitches. As you might have guessed, this is a mirroring technique and requires a certain level of mindfulness. Done correctly, it will unconsciously build rapport. Match the speaker's energy as best as you can and follow your instincts when it comes to mimicry so you can avoid coming off as annoying. Something else you might notice while trying out this mirror technique is what a person is experiencing. You might even realize that the person is suffering from a medical condition just by monitoring their breath. For example, if it's excruciating to breathe as slowly as the speaker due to the long pauses in between the inhales and exhales, then you might be speaking with a hypothyroid patient. If it's incredibly stressful to breathe as fast as the speaker, you might be speaking with a hypersensitive person. In either case, you realize there's more to their demeanor and temperament than meets the eye. That helps to build on your empathy and avoid overreacting to them.

- Recognize cognitive dissonance and detach from it when that's appropriate

Have you ever heard a pianist hit six adjacent keys at the same time? Dissonance is the word we use for that kind of sound. It can be very off-putting. When communicating, we want to avoid dissonance and strive for harmony. But sometimes, we are hit with cognitive dissonance during a conversation. It's usually when we think about two things that can't be true at the same time. Cognitive dissonance can make it hard to hear facts that conflict with our pre-conceptions. One way to deal with cognitive dissonance healthily is to remember that statements can be valid on several different levels. Some of the things people tell us are very close to what we'd say if we were in their position. When someone tells you something that seems improbable to you, empathetic listening encourages you to switch on your curiosity and try to figure out and understand why they would say it.

Sometimes listening to dissonant information provides much-needed information. When experimenter Russell Targ described himself on the front cover of a book as "A Blind Biker," readers expected him to say that he'd been a biker before becoming blind. This statement repelled non-readers because they couldn't accept it as true. Those who actually read the book discovered that there's a technology that made it possible for a very near-sighted (legally blind) person to ride a motorbike.

And here's one more thing I want to point out—all babies barely make sense when they learn to talk. But somehow, we don't let that annoy us because we've accepted that kind of dissonance. Granted, most people don't expect babies to make much sense, and I am in no way suggesting you think of adults as babies, but merely pointing out that you have the ability to handle some dissonance without losing your cool.

- Give the speaker the benefit of the doubt as they express themselves

At the start of this book, I pointed out that few will think and act like you. It's important to remember that when engaged in conversation. As an active listener, your intention shouldn't be to fit the speaker's viewpoint into yours, as that rarely works. Instead, you want to see things from the speaker's point of view. Most of the time, their belief will conflict with yours, and that's okay. It would be best if you still embraced them as unique individuals free to express their perspective. So, give the speaker the benefit of the doubt and ask questions if you must to help you reconcile this difference. Listening with empathy requires some self-control and a lot of awareness, as you may have realized. Your ego will want to shut down anything that doesn't align with your belief system. Your brain will tend to take in a few words, then leap ahead in judgment, eager to fire back an equally harsh response. That is when you need to hold your tongue. Pause mentally and give yourself time to THINK!

Chapter 6: Five Levels of Communication and the Ego

"Most people do not listen with the intent to understand. Most people listen with the intent to reply." — Stephen Covey

Communication between humans occurs on numerous levels simultaneously. We've covered some of the levels, but I want us to consolidate what you've learned so you can start intentionally applying it to your life. The five levels through which you need to start communicating to influence desired outcomes are verbally, physically, auditorily, emotionally, and energetically.

Verbally

This level is, of course, the most apparent one. You probably chose this book because you realize you need to improve on this level. To do so, you must begin by increasing your vocabulary and getting more intentional with your word choice in relation to the listener. Most of the words in the English dictionary can have different meanings. Different words also evoke different memories, meanings, and imagery for each of us.

That's why knowing your audience is vital, so you can relate to their worldview as much as possible. For example, if you're trying to establish rapport with someone from Japan, giving stories or metaphors that people from Texas enjoy will probably fall flat. Similarly, if you're trying to get your point across to your new girlfriend, bringing up your ex-fiancée will likely evoke the wrong imagery. As Aristotle once said, "To communicate effectively on the verbal level, select the "right" words and usage for the context of the conversation."

In other words, keep in mind the person's moral, ethnic, and religious preference as well as any bias they might be holding.

Physically

We communicate physically through visual cues, including eye contact, gestures, movements, stances, breathing, posture, and facial expressions. If you want to become a more effective communicator and establish trust quickly, it's helpful if you can align with others. Connect with them in form and movement. Notice how they move their upper body, the words they frequently use, and the pace they keep. It is also helpful to become mindful of your posture, facial expressions, and hand gestures.

Neuro-linguistic programming (NLP) has increased our awareness of the importance of understanding the signals and messages we send out through these mediums. When used with integrity, techniques like mirroring and matching people's posture, gestures, and words can increase the receptivity of your message.

Auditory

The next level of communicating that matters is the sound of your voice, including tone, range, volume, and speed. As the speaker, you need to intentionally manipulate your voice to support the strength and intensity of your message while also being cautious to avoid sending the wrong signals to the listener. For example, if you're passing on a cautionary statement, your words should be concise and straightforward with no ambiguity. Your tone of voice shouldn't be too harsh or too soft because either option will lead to undesirable interpretations.

Take notice of how you inflect, enunciate, and emphasize certain words because that may impact how others interpret the meaning of your message. If you want to improve your communication at this level, invest some time listening to others and notice how they vary their pitch and tone. Listen to great political speakers and your own people as they speak and notice how they speak when sharing important news. That can enable you to match and mirror that same tone, making it easier for them to receive your news since you'll be speaking in their preferred manner.

Emotionally

In life, we tend to assume that we can separate emotions and logic. We think that emotions play no role in the decision-making process in a business context or that it doesn't impact how a conversation goes.

A clear example is when a salesperson walks into a meeting to sell a prospect his product. If the salesman doesn't consider the emotional factor involved in communicating and decision-making, he will likely lose the sale. The same is true in any interaction. The listening party will always filter whatever message is being passed through their emotional lens. Think about your personality for a second—are you more receptive to someone with a great enthusiastic attitude or someone who is negative and condescending? If an individual walked into the room and the first thing they said with a grim look on their face was, "You idiot, I have been looking everywhere for you. I've got some important news to give you!" what would your immediate reaction be? Do you think that interaction would go well? Now switch scenarios for a moment and imagine yourself in the same room, but this time, someone walks in with a big smile on their face, and they say, "Good morning sir/madam, I come bearing some important news that you'll want to hear. I'm glad I found you here." Which approach stirs up your logic and emotions in a positive and receptive way?

If you want to improve your communication with others at an emotional level, increase your self-awareness. Learn to pause and do a self-check internally before attempting to connect with others so that you can always meet them with positive energy. Notice your tendency when you begin an interaction. Is there a sense of judgment or criticism? Do you feel insecure, angry, fearful? Whatever you feel will influence your communication.

Trust me, the energy you bring will impact how receptive they are to your news.

Energetically

This level of communication requires less than ordinary thinking. It involves accessing many unseen factors, including a person's level of consciousness, the frequency of harmonics of the message, and other subtle energies. Although it sounds complicated, it's actually very natural for your mind to do as long as the awareness is there.

Have you noticed how some people just seem to have an "X-factor" about them? Think of Obama (former president of the United States) and how he seemed to have this unique presence that made others listen and openly receive his ideas. Whether you support his political views or not is beside the point. Learn from what he demonstrates as a master communicator.

If you'd like to communicate more effectively with others, you need to develop that same quality of holding the highest intention for others. It's not enough to develop your skills. You also need to develop empathy and a genuine interest in the people you want to influence. That will require a higher level of mindfulness and insight. A good starting point if you're going to begin your journey of mastery is mindfulness practices.

Bringing These Five Levels of Communication Together

The way you express yourself represents your beliefs, thoughts, and the message you wish to convey. All the levels that were mentioned above influence each other and affect how the listener interprets your communication.

For instance, your emotional state impacts your physical state and tone of voice even if you're using the right words. So if internally, you're criticizing and holding the listener in a less than optimal light, you don't need to outright call him a moron. He will feel it even if your words are "kind." The unsaid and unspoken aspect of your communication is just as loud as what you're speaking.

Therefore, you must work on aligning all these five levels. Become more aware of your gestures, posture, the words you chose, the tone and cadence of your conversation, and how you feel about the audience.

The 5 C's of Effective Communication

It's time to master the five C's of communication: clarity, cohesiveness, completeness, conciseness, and concreteness.

#1. Clarity

Clarity is about getting your thoughts together and thinking through what you will say to impact and influence the listener. It's essential for trust-building. Whether it's a formal or casual interaction, I encourage you to always think through what you want to say or write. The more people feel like they understand you, the easier it will be to take the desired action.

#2. Cohesiveness

When communicating with someone, use a logical path that your listener can follow. Lead the person from point A (the start of the communication) to point B (the main point they should take away) clearly and easily. If you digress or meander, you will confuse and lose your listener's attention, so maintain focus and purpose.

#3. Completeness

Have you ever been in a conversation with someone who started a sentence right in the middle, and then halfway through that explanation, they switched to an entirely new and irrelevant story? That can be very annoying and meaningless to the person on the receiving end. While it is okay to create some cliffhangers and open-ended questions, make sure you always complete and conclude your message.

Depending on the particular context, you might even want to summarize what you just shared or directly call your audience to action.

#4. Conciseness

When looking to influence and impact your listener, conciseness matters. Make each word count. You do this by carefully constructing what you will say beforehand. Don't be one of those people who throws out each and every thought that pops up as they speak. Instead, take your time, use precise words that deliver the meaning you intend, and avoid redundancy. For example, most teens will be all too familiar with the phrase "I'm only going to say this once," which is usually followed by a never-ending lecture. Perhaps you've been in a meeting with someone who can't seem to shut up and takes half an hour to make a point that they could have made in five minutes.

A few tips on how to be more concise include knowing when to shut up, avoiding getting distracted mid-speech by issues and ideas that aren't relevant to your main point, and using talk-ending techniques. You should also ask someone you trust for some feedback on the volume of words you use so that you can get in the habit of using just the right amount. Remember, it's not about skipping important information for the sake of brevity; instead, it's about picking the right words to convey all that you need to pass on.

#5. Concreteness

The last tip is to avoid being ambiguous with your communication. If you leave room for alternative interpretations, there's a higher chance of miscommunication. The English language can be notoriously vague, so it's especially critical that you use the proper terminology and even share some examples with your audience if necessary. For example, if you need someone to complete a task that you just assigned them, never say "I need that report soon, John," because soon is very abstract. John might not prioritize it, and a month later, you might still be yelling for the report. Even saying "I need the report within the month" is still ambiguous and open to several interpretations. So, the best way to communicate would be to ask John to hand in the report by 11 am on the 3rd of April. See the difference?

If you're married or in a committed relationship, this skill is vital. Don't just tell your spouse to "help out with the dishes" or "take out the trash." Your partner can interpret those messages in ten different ways. Be concrete with your request and let them know precisely when and how often you would like this assistance. That will minimize any delays or misunderstandings.

Chapter 7: It All Starts with You

"Those who cannot change their minds cannot change anything." — George Bernard Shaw

All your activities hinge on your ability to connect with and develop deep relationships. You cannot advance in most careers, sell a house or product, pitch a story, marry your ideal partner, etc., without this ability to connect with others in a healthy way. And while human interactions are complex, the one thing you can bank on is that you're already setting yourself up for success by working on yourself.

Chances are, you know someone who is really great at making others feel important. That person can get others to do things they wouldn't otherwise. When this person makes a request, people gladly oblige and even volunteer to go out of their way to help them. That's a simple illustration of positive influence over others. But if you want to be the same, you're going to have to learn some universal principles that help build healthy relationships. While it might be easy to assume someone with positive influence is just good at "getting what they want from others," the deeper and often hidden truth is that it takes a person who has developed certain qualities to become a positive influence on others. Much of the work required is internal. The qualities you would need to develop include:

- Generosity

You can become more generous with your praise as a foundation for all your relationships. People always perform better and receive your message with more openness and humility when you approach them with approval and generosity.

- A genuine interest in other people

If you can train yourself to remember people's names, ask them questions that encourage them to talk about themselves so you can learn more about what makes them tick. People love talking about their interests, passions, and even dislikes which are all useful when you start communicating.

- Humility and owning your mistakes

It may seem counterintuitive and challenging for your ego but developing this quality will transform your life. When you become humble and reasonable enough to admit your mistakes, the person involved will be less defensive, disagreeable, and judgmental. It helps end tension swiftly and even shows the other person your "humanness," which builds connection.

- Listen...I mean, really listen

You are the one who must take the first step and become a great listener. Seek to understand others and invest your attention and energy in reading other people as they communicate with you. Listen to what is spoken and what is left unsaid. Therein lies the explanation for what people need in order to feel validated, supported, and seen.

A mother once told me, "I don't know what's wrong with my daughter. I can't understand why she won't listen to me at all."

I paused for a moment and said, "Let me restate what you just said. You don't understand your daughter because she won't listen to you?"

"That's right," the mother replied.

"Let me try again," I said. "You don't understand your daughter because she won't listen to you?"

"That's what I just said," she replied with some agitation.

"I thought that to understand another person, you needed to do the listening," I suggested.

This time, there was a long pause from the mother. "Oh!" she said. "*Oh!*" she said again as the light bulb went on. "Oh yeah, you're right, and I do understand her. I know what she's going through. I went through the same thing when I was her age. I guess what I don't understand is why she won't listen to me."

That is a classic example of a parent who has no idea of what's really going on inside her daughter's head. She was too much in her own head, projecting her thoughts and viewpoint of the world, and totally missed seeing her daughter's. Most of us are the same in our interactions. We are so filled with our own assumptions and assertions it becomes challenging to have a genuine interaction or even communicate effectively. Then we think it's the other person at fault.

That's why in this chapter, we want to bring the awareness that real conversations begin with you. It's on you to make the paradigm shift needed to transform monologues into dialogues. And that can only happen when you take a real interest in understanding other human beings before you demand to be understood. In an earlier chapter, we touched on empathic listening. Let's take that introduction a step further by learning how to develop it for yourself.

Listening with the Intent to Understand

Empathic (from empathy) listening is more than active listening. It's about seeing things from the other person's frame of reference. You look out through their lens to see the world as they do and understand their operating paradigm without judgment.

This doesn't mean that you agree with the person or even justify their behavior. It simply means you feel what they feel and respect that they have that right, too. You gain accurate data to work with through empathic listening, so you don't need to judge or assume. It also prevents you from projecting your own beliefs and motives because you're listening with your head and heart. As you listen, you receive information through their words, facial expressions, behavior, and emotional cues. As you can see, building rapport and effectively communicating involves just as much listening as it does speaking. The starting point is learning to tame your mind and discipline your focus so you can be fully present to listen with empathy.

Developing Empathy

People who don't exhibit empathy will often come across as cold and self-absorbed, no matter how great they are at communicating. Conversely, someone who is empathetic always comes across as warm and caring. People are more receptive and trusting even if the person isn't a strong communicator. That's why you need to engage in some practices that increase your empathy.

#1: Engage your heart, not just your head. Get into the habit of reading books and materials that explore personal relationships and emotions. I know it might feel awkward or too soft at first, but research shows this activity improves empathy.

#2: Examine your biases. We all have biases that interfere with our ability to communicate effectively. These are often centered around visible factors such as race, gender, age, corporate rank, social status, etc. Do you think you have active biases hindering your ability to communicate with someone you've been struggling to get through to? Think again. The chances are high that you have a lot of biases because we all do. What matters is that we become more aware and adequately deal with them as they show up. Instead of allowing your prejudices to build walls, seek commonalities that can bring you and the other person into closer connection and collaboration.

#3: Increase your curiosity. Everyone has something to teach you and some value to add to your life. Yes, even that person that you assume is a complete moron. What can you learn from that so-called idiot who doesn't listen to you? What can that angry, demanding client help you understand about yourself? Curious people ask lots of questions and keep a very open mind to continue developing a stronger understanding of the people around them. That, in turn, creates stronger connections.

Chapter 8: Emotional Intelligence

"If you are tuned out of your emotions, you will be poor at reading them in other people." — *Daniel Goleman*

You may have heard of the acronym EQ, which stands for emotional quotient. But have you heard of EI?

Emotional Intelligence (EI) has become a trending topic, especially among leaders, as our society increases awareness. For years, having a high EQ was considered the defining factor for a perfect leader. Today, things have changed. Leaders with high emotional intelligence seem to be the most valued and highly respected people. You don't need to be the leader of an organization to develop high EI. In fact, I think every human being on this planet will have a better experience interacting with fellow humans as they improve and develop their emotional intelligence. In relation to effectively communicating with others and building trust, emotional intelligence matters a lot more than being the most intelligent person in the room. But what exactly is emotional intelligence, and why is it important?

Emotional Intelligence Simplified

Emotional intelligence comprises a wide array of skills, but at its core is the ability to perceive, control, and evaluate emotions. We are all emotional creatures, such is the nature of the human species, but some of us are better at managing said emotions than others. Is that an inborn talent or a skill that one develops on their own?

It depends on who you ask. Some believe emotional intelligence is a characteristic one is born with. Others think it can be learned. I don't think it matters. What's important is the realization that your emotions impact every facet of your life. How you communicate with others and how they perceive you are both influenced by your feelings. The more you can understand and interpret your emotions in a healthy way, the easier it will be to interpret other people's emotions. Some psychologists suggest that emotional intelligence can be more important than your IQ in your quest for success.

The Four Domains of Emotional Intelligence

- Self-awareness

Self-awareness is the big one. It's the first step to improving or developing your emotional intelligence. In this domain, the focus is on perceiving and understanding emotions accurately, which can only happen if you have greater awareness. It also includes understanding nonverbal signals like body language and facial expressions.

- Self-management

Self-management includes emotional self-control, adaptability, achievement orientation, and a positive outlook. This level involves using your emotions in a healthy way to promote thinking and cognitive activity. How you pay attention and react to things around you will determine how good you are at emotional self-regulation and management.

- Social awareness

Social awareness includes empathy and organizational awareness. At this level, you can now expand your EI beyond your emotions to perceive others. If someone is expressing angry feelings, you as the observer must interpret the cause of the person's anger and what it could mean. If your emotional intelligence level is high, you would accurately make that interpretation. For instance, if your boss is acting angry, instead of taking it personally and getting angry too, you could try to understand the reason they are behaving this way. Perhaps they got a speeding ticket on their way to work or had a morning fight with their spouse. By understanding the context and cause behind another person's emotions, you are better equipped to respond to their unpleasant behavior.

- Relationship management

Relationship management includes influence, conflict management, teamwork, inspirational leadership, coaching, and mentoring. It's also about managing the relationship you have with yourself. The ability to control how you react and how quickly you regulate your emotions under stressful or uncomfortable situations is key in relationship building. Improving your emotional intelligence will enable you to respond appropriately to others even when their emotions are out of control.

I have a friend named Dave who has been working on his emotional intelligence for several years. He manages a team of forty people at their company. "There is never a dull day," Dave likes to say to me whenever we meet up for coffee. Recently he shared a story of how one of his guys messed up on a project, and the head of another department caught sight of the mishap. It derailed that department as well, and naturally, she stormed into Dave's office about to explode with anger. She yelled and screamed and described all the ways Dave and his team were useless, calling them all kinds of names. Dave sat in silence and called upon every inch of self-control he could find. Finally, after seeing him sitting there silent and paying attention to her grievance, she collapsed on the chair across from him and broke down into tears. Dave said, "I'm really sorry we messed up. I already have my guy fixing the issue, and you'll have it at your desk by the end of the day delivered personally by me. But I have to ask, is everything okay with you, Shelly?"

It turns out Shelly was having a dreadful week. Lots of personal problems and things not going her way had been mounting up within her. This morning she had that final trigger that caused her to throw a temper tantrum. In the end, Dave was able to not only calm her down but also practiced everything he'd been learning about being a better leader. Sometimes, even our bosses require us to take the lead. But we need emotional intelligence to do that.

What Level Are You At?

You will find various tests online that help you measure your emotional intelligence. These assessments generally fall into two types, namely, self-report tests and ability tests.

Self-report tests offer you questions or statements that you respond to. In other words, you rate your own behavior and, in the end, get a score that helps you recognize your current levels. An example of this would be the statement, "I often feel that I understand how others are feeling." Here you would be asked to either disagree, somewhat disagree, agree, or strongly agree.

Ability tests involve responding to situations and then getting your skills assessed and rated by a third party. An example of this would be to take an emotional intelligence test administered by a mental health professional. The most common approaches used by health professionals are:

a. The Mayer-Salovey-Caruso Emotional Intelligence Test (MSCEIT) measures the four branches of Mayer and Salovey's EI model. In this test, you perform tasks designed to assess your ability to perceive, identify, understand, and manage emotions.

b. Emotional and Social Competence Inventory (ESCI) involves getting people who know you well to rate your abilities in several different emotional competencies. The test evaluates social and emotional abilities that help distinguish strong leaders from everyone else. Although it's an old tool, many still prefer it. You can find many more tools and options online, so keep investigating if you'd like to take an ability test.

Why You Want to Develop Your Emotional Intelligence

Patrick is a well-liked manager of a small team. He is kind, respectful, and tries to be sensitive to the needs of others. Patrick is a great problem solver and always sees setbacks as opportunities waiting to be seized. He is always a source of calm to his colleagues and tries to be as engaging as he can. Although on many accounts, he is a great boss to have (and others tell him that), Patrick is starting to feel stuck because he can see that he's not getting through with as much impact as he would like. His bosses also don't seem to value his likable personality and positive outlook. Patrick recognizes that emotional intelligence is one of his strong suits, but he's starting to think it doesn't matter as much when it comes to developing trust and advancing one's career. Sure, people are happy to listen to him, but they don't really take action on what he says.

Patrick doesn't realize that emotional intelligence isn't just about being likable, sensitive, and social. Critical elements are missing from his understanding of emotional intelligence, which I just outlined. So, when it comes to improving your EI, you need to make sure you're holistically hitting all four domains. When you do, you'll notice various internal and external shifts taking place, including but not limited to:

- The natural ability to think before reacting

As you become an emotionally intelligent person, you will find yourself creating a buffer time before responding to anything someone says or does, no matter how highly charged the situation may be. If you recall the story my friend Dave shared, he was able to summon enough self-control to stay calm and let Shelly have her little tantrum. Was it easy? Not at all. It took a lot of discipline and willpower to shut up and not react when she attacked him and his team. However, Dave now understands that emotions are powerful and temporary. If he can allow himself a little buffer time before responding, he is more likely to be calmer, more in control of his emotions and the hot situation. The same will become of you as you improve your EI.

• Increased self-awareness

If there's one gift we all need, it must be greater self-awareness. The more you know yourself, the more you can understand others and handle them accordingly. Self-awareness allows us to consider many different factors before reacting to anything. A lot has been written on the Internet regarding self-awareness, what it is, and why it makes us better human beings. Feel free to study it a bit more. *Greater Good* magazine from the Greater Good Science Center has done a lot of research and surveys on self-awareness.

Coming back to Patrick's story—he felt at a loss because he lacked enough self-awareness to realize the critical elements he was missing, including the ability to have tough conversations, give negative feedback, and constructively accepting criticism without getting defensive.

- Empathy

Empathy has become a buzzword. It's easy for us to lose sight of its importance simply because we see it everywhere. We already discussed empathic listening, and as you may have guessed, that skill emerges from having this quality of empathy. Emotional intelligence will help you strengthen and develop your empathy, making you an empathic listener.

How to Improve Your Emotional Intelligence for Better Conversations

#1: Reflect

Observing and assessing your own emotions is an essential aspect of emotional intelligence. Invest some time to reflect on your own feelings and consider how they influence your decisions and behaviors. When you're thinking about how other people respond, assess the role that their emotions play. Ask yourself often, "Why am I feeling this way? Are there any unseen factors that might be contributing to these feelings?"

When interacting with others, be mindful of their emotions, and as you observe their reactions, you can ask yourself questions such as "Why is this person feeling this way? Are there any unseen factors that might be contributing to these feelings? How do my emotions differ from this person's emotions?"

Explore these questions with an open mind. Allow your awareness of yourself and others to increase. Sooner or later, you will find it easier to understand the role that emotions play in how people think and behave.

#2: Stop reacting and start responding in the face of conflict

During instances of conflict, emotional outbursts like what we saw between Dave and Shelly are fairly common. They usually drive both parties into states of anger, distress, and reactiveness. If, however, one of the people involved is accustomed to practicing emotional intelligence, the conflict can be quickly resolved without further damage. You need to become an emotionally intelligent person in all your interactions. How? By training your brain to stop reacting to a conflict. Stay calm regardless of how distressed you might feel. Know that it's okay to feel that impulse, but if you can gain control over your brain, you can hit pause long enough to calm yourself and respond more productively. That will help you avoid worsening the situation. Understand that in times of conflict, the goal is to resolve the situation. Make a conscious choice to focus on ensuring your actions and words align with the outcome you most desire.

#3: Work on your attitude

Never underestimate the power of a positive attitude. Most of us don't realize how pessimistic and judgmental we are. You might be a great and enthusiastic person around your friends, but who you are when delivering tough news, negative feedback, or trying to get your team to perform better speaks volumes. That's what determines how effective your communication will be. If you're often pessimistic around co-workers or strangers, it's going to be hard to build a strong rapport because your attitude will be like an unpleasant perfume that everyone around you can smell. Some of the things you can do to improve your attitude include engaging in mindset developing activities like reading a good self-help book, hiring a coach, meditating during the day, keeping positive quotes at your desk or computer, etc.

#4: Practice self-awareness

Engage in exercises and activities that make you more aware of your physical, mental, emotional, and spiritual aspects. In other words, do everything you can to "Know Thyself." You must become aware of all your emotions and how they affect those around you. Become aware of the most dominant emotions that stick around for most of the day. As you learn to tune into your own feelings, you'll develop the ability to tune into other people's emotions, raising your empathy and emotional intelligence.

Nine Signs You Have a High Emotional Intelligence

#1: You are an assertive communicator

When you have high levels of emotional intelligence, you're not just good at passing out compliments and praise. You're also courageous and confident enough to address conflict, concerns, and other people's needs in a calm, straightforward way. By the way, this is a strong suit when it comes to building rapport and establishing trust because people recognize your authenticity.

#2: You're curious about people

If you are naturally curious about humans, human emotions, and why people behave as they do, that is a sign of emotional intelligence. You can be introverted, extroverted, or anything in between but the fact that you care about other people and what they are feeling or going through demonstrates that you have a lot of empathy, which is a crucial aspect of emotional intelligence.

#3: You are aware of your strengths and weaknesses

Self-awareness plays a huge role in helping you determine what you're good at and where you need some improvements. It's not just about understanding emotions. It's also about knowing the skills that you're good at and the ones you struggle with. Having a high emotional intelligence means you know how to lean into your strengths and use them to your full advantage while keeping your weaknesses from holding you back.

#4: You don't get offended easily

How quick are you to get defensive when someone says something snarky? If you are the type of person who is difficult to offend, then you likely have really high emotional intelligence. Think of it as developing thick, impenetrable skin. Perhaps you're the kind of person who will even laugh at yourself when you make a silly mistake and allow a humorous joke about your personality slide because you can mentally draw the line between humor and degradation.

#5: You let go of mistakes and setbacks

Suppose you had a tense moment earlier in the day. Do you carry on that heavy heart to every meeting and interaction? If you have high levels of emotional intelligence, then you know how to process the setbacks and unpleasant experiences that show up. So, if you happened to get yelled at or fight with a spouse, friend, or colleague, train yourself to say, "Okay, that moment is over now, I am going into my next meeting totally different, and I am leaving all that drama at the door!" That obviously entails having enough self-awareness and emotional regulation so you can manage your energy and how you show up better.

#6: You don't hold grudges

When we hold on to an upsetting remark or a grudge, we usually trigger stress hormones. That becomes counterproductive to the health of any relationship or communication. It impacts your ability to communicate with the other person and puts your health at risk. According to recent findings, holding on to stress wreaks havoc on your body and can have devastating long-term effects. Researchers at Emory University have shown that holding onto stress can contribute to heart disease, high blood pressure, and other fatal diseases. So, you need to learn to avoid this at all costs. Suppose you're the type of person who easily lets go of grudges and cuts off all need for resentment. In that case, it's mainly because you're operating at high levels of empathy and emotional intelligence.

#7: You embrace change

How does change make you feel? For most people, change is associated with stress and anxiety. Many people fear and resist change, but few (those who are emotionally intelligent) are able to carry a different perspective. These individuals remain flexible and tend to adapt quickly where others get stuck and paralyzed. That leads to a lot of unhappiness. On the contrary, people with high levels of emotional intelligence seek out change, and when they sense it coming, immediately form a plan of action to help them manage the change when it comes.

#8: You have a robust emotional vocabulary

The spectrum of emotions, both positive and negative, is vast. Emotionally intelligent people don't need to master all of them, but they understand the most basic ones when they show up in themselves and others. These individuals can accurately identify and name most of the emotions they encounter. Surprisingly, research shows only 36% of people can effectively do this. So, if you're good at identifying your feelings, you likely have high levels of emotional intelligence. If not, it's time to shift that because unlabeled emotions usually create a lot of misunderstanding, irrational choices, and unproductive actions.

A key benefit of learning to name your emotions is that it enables you to become better acquainted with them. You don't just settle for "I feel bad." Instead, you can state, "I'm feeling irritable/frustrated/anxious." When you can name the emotion, you can tame the emotion because you'll know exactly what to do to make things better.

#9: You're good at identifying and neutralizing toxic people

This one is hard for most people to do, except those that are emotionally intelligent. Are you often the one people call when they need a resolution? Do you find yourself able to handle even the nastiest people in a room? If so, then you can consider yourself an emotionally intelligent individual.

Think back to Dave's story. He neutralized Shelly and even got her to open up about what was really bothering her. That's what you should aim to develop as well if it has been missing thus far. It requires the ability to keep your feelings in check not through suppression but through awareness and conscious regulation. If you still need to work on this some more, here's what to do: Identify the emotion, breathe deeply, and don't allow your anger or frustration to fuel the ongoing situation. Consider for a moment the other person's point of view. See if you can find common ground. If the person is too toxic and you feel like there's nothing to be done, then refrain from engaging their ego. Simply find a way to remove yourself from that experience and avoid allowing that person to enter and run into your mental space.

Chapter 9: Getting Through to Others

"To effectively communicate, we must realize that we are all different in the way we perceive the world and use this understanding as a guide to our communication with others."
— *Tony Robbins*

Have you ever felt like you are speaking, but no one is listening? Worse still, have you recognized bored listening, tired listening, or even hostile listening as you addressed your audience? You intuitively knew they didn't understand a word you said, and you were not on the same page, which only increased your frustration. Statistically speaking, it happens a lot because most humans aren't very good at active listening.

Since we've established most people are bad at listening, you should never engage in any conversation (especially the ones that matter to you) without asking yourself this: "What is the listening I'm speaking into?" In other words, what filters do I have to deal with here? Everyone has their own life experiences, and that creates filters that will impact what they hear. Effective communication is about becoming more aware of that fact so that you can understand the other person's dynamic process. Instead of approaching it with a linear perspective, see it as a dynamic circle. In truth, it is a circle because the way you speak affects the way your audience listens and the way your audience listens affects the way you speak.

Consider Your Audience

Before you speak:
1. Consider who you'll be addressing. Whether it's one individual or a group, you need to think ahead of time about how you will approach them for the best possible outcome.
2. Think about what they want to hear.
3. Consider their cultural background and some of the filters they might have that would cause them to interpret your words in one way instead of another.

For example, if you're talking to your wife or girlfriend about a sensitive issue that you know she's self-conscious about, make an effort to choose words that will cause her to feel understood and respected.

The same is true if you're talking to a colleague who has been struggling with performance or personal issues lately. If you're meeting a new client and you don't have a lot of information on them, it might be helpful to ask a few questions at the beginning of the talk to gain a basic understanding of who they are.

I once attended a seminar meant to last an entire weekend, but I was gone after the end of the first day. Why? Because throughout the first morning and afternoon sessions, I felt the speaker was only focused on himself. He spoke in references and anecdotes that meant nothing to me. His speech was more like a monologue than an interactive workshop. It just felt to me like I had wasted my money to spend a weekend with a guy in a shiny suit standing on stage who loved being in the spotlight. He didn't seem to care at all about us (his audience and clients), and I could see everyone in that room struggled to understand what his expensive-looking PowerPoint presentation was about. Had this "out of state" business guru done his homework better, he would have been able to adjust his speech, anecdotes, and PowerPoint to better suit what we were accustomed to. Then perhaps his metaphors would have been life-changing.

Something I have seen great speakers do is continually adjust to match their audience. If the crowd is older, change your pace and cultural reference. If you're speaking abroad where people are different, slow down and take long pauses when you make an important point. Small things make all the difference when it comes to getting through to people.

Six Ways to Get People to Listen to You

#1: Hone your Emotional Intelligence

Your end goal is to build trust and develop deeper connections which means getting others to listen and relate to you is critical. But before you can do that, you really need to start by honing what we talked about earlier—your emotional intelligence. Bringing empathy into the conversation ensures you have more successful communication. Never underestimate the power of kindness and empathy. As you show people respect, you are more likely to genuinely receive the same.

A practical technique you can apply here is to ask yourself: How would this person I'm trying to get through to want this framed? What have they been positively responsive to in the past?

#2: Use silence as a strategy

Silence can be powerful in helping your message sink in deeper. Make good use of long pauses when you've articulated an important point. That gives you a chance to read the room, listen in for reactions, and it keeps you mindful and present. If engaged in a heated discussion, taking this pause allows you to take a few deep breaths and buffer your reaction, which will help you avoid impulsive reactions and emotional outbursts.

#3: Build genuine relationships with those you want to influence

The most impactful and beloved leaders are those who have mastered their interpersonal skills. They invest time to know their employees, remember names, and always make whomever they interact with feel special. Because they take the time and make an effort to know the people around them, others naturally pay full attention. Getting through to others and influencing them in any way is about earning that right. The more credible you are, the easier it will be to receive the respect and attention you deserve.

#4: Be more mindful of how you carry yourself

People largely decide whether or not to listen to you based on how you carry yourself. Your body language, the vocabulary and tone you use, and how you dress can make a difference. Knowing this, make sure you're thinking about these different aspects so you can represent yourself in the best way possible. If you're a parent who drinks, yells, and creates drama around the house each weekend, it's going to be tough getting through to your teenage son, who sneaks out on Friday nights to "hang out with his friends past curfew." You can punish them all you want, yell and force them to sit and listen to your whining lectures, but it doesn't mean they'll shift behavior because based on how you carry yourself, it's hard for them to see you as that highly respectable parental figure.

#5: Get out of your own way

Most of the time, we get too caught up in our own thinking. We forget that getting through to others is about being invested in them, not how you sound in your head. This kind of self-consciousness is actually unhealthy and creates a wall between you and the listener. Don't turn your communication into a self-validating, self-focused monologue if you want to get through to someone. Instead, focus entirely on the audience. Be a giver and leave the person feeling like investing their attention on you was worthwhile.

#6: Increase your confidence

A timid, shy person who stumbles over their words will never garner the attention they need, and neither will an overly aggressive person. Most of the time, these expressions are off-putting for our brains. We might sit through that conversation, but it doesn't mean we're listening, much less influenced by the listener. Unconsciously we can sense something is "off" with the person. That's why you really need to build your confidence and self-esteem. We'll talk more about this in the next chapter. The critical thing to note is you need to have high confidence levels to communicate and build rapport with others effectively.

Chapter 10: The Art of Connecting with Others

"I've learned that people will forget what you said, people will forget what you did, but people will never forget how you made them feel." — Maya Angelou

The reason you picked this book isn't just because you wanted to learn how to build trust but because you want to know how to build trust with those who are "different" from you. It's easy to develop a connection with someone who thinks like you and shares similar values and mannerisms. What's not so easy is having a successful and impactful conversation with a person who shares different values and worldviews. You're not alone in this struggle, but the good news is, there is an art to improving your current state. It just requires some adjustments on your end so you can integrate the attitudes, beliefs, and behaviors that will help you connect more effectively with those different from you.

Be present in the moment and make others feel valued.

The great psychologist Abraham Maslow, famed for his "hierarchy of needs," placed the need to belong on the second rung making "survival" the only other important thing to us as human beings. The more you can help people feel like they belong as you engage with them, the easier it will be to get through to them. Listening is a major component of developing a connection. The more you practice empathy and active listening, the more the other person will feel a bond with you. You also need to be present as you share that moment with the other person, whether you're talking or listening. You might also be under the false assumption that a connection can only happen when you're happy, positive, and sharing good news. Actually, you can create an equally strong bond when you're open and vulnerable enough to share uncomfortable or sad news.

I once heard of a story about a man and his newly divorced wife who went through a tragic experience. Their only child had an accident, and they both spent hours in the hospital anxious, stressed, and worried for him. That experience actually brought them closer as the wife saw a side of her husband she had never experienced. She realized he wasn't just a selfish, inconsiderate workaholic. The man also saw his ex in a new way realizing how strong and reliable she is. At the end of the year, they got back together and soon renewed their vows for the second time. What can this teach us? Even sad, traumatic, and negative experiences can bring us closer to the person we want to develop a connection with as long as we have enough courage to be vulnerable and authentic.

Do you find connecting with other people hard? Have you been feeling like you're not making the impact or deep connection you'd like to have with others? You likely need to reflect on yourself more closely. Are there any childhood traumas or personality disorders that stand in the way? Do you have trust issues? Is your self-esteem low? These are a few of the reasons you might be struggling to form a connection, and they need to be addressed. Once you've worked on yourself, it's time to start investing in getting to know others and what they want.

Know Who You Are Dealing With

There's a difference between the act of connecting and the art of connecting. The act of connecting involves good listening and verbal skills. In contrast, the art of connecting adds a deeper layer to that by including curiosity, respect, and seeking commonalities even where they seem to be lacking.

Before you can develop a deep connection with someone, you need to identify their values, cultural preferences, and interests you might have in common. Although we often think of culture as existing within communities, companies, and families, there's also an existing culture in individual relationships. The beauty of culture between individuals is that it often has less of a downside than that of groups or communities.

When I'm forming a friendship or connection with someone, we create unspoken rules about our relationship in a dynamic way. With each conversation and each shared experience, I get to learn more, discover more, and invest more into that relationship which forms a bond. Over time, this allows for a deep organic connection that works even if we don't agree on all matters.

The culture created in a two-way relationship will be far more nuanced and open than a culture attached to an identity. It allows differences to exist without them hindering the growth of that relationship. But of course, it takes work on your part to create that kind of magic. The more you can invest in understanding the person you want to form a connection with, the easier it will be to develop this.

How to Start Developing a Connection

• Take the initiative and invest in getting to know the other person

This should come as no surprise, really, given how much emphasis we've placed on your taking the lead in order to become an effective listener. Before you engage in conversation:

1. Do a little research about the person. If it's someone you already know, make it a point to greet them warmly and with a renewed sense of curiosity.
2. Be genuinely interested without being creepy or intrusive.
3. Ask questions about their family, interests, background, needs, hobbies, and current work.
4. See if you can build up to the point where you naturally feel like getting together for another conversation.

• Demonstrate genuine care

Show the person that you do actually care about their ideas, opinions, and well-being. If you can find something to appreciate, affirm, or praise, be sure to do so. Recognize their accomplishments, and when it comes to giving constructive feedback or talking about a mistake that the person made, do it with compassion, kindness, and truth.

- Provide massive help

Everyone has something they'd like some help with. Be that person who is always ready and eager to help wherever you can. Too many people never reach out and connect with someone they want to because they fear rejection. If that's you, I have great news. You can quickly build rapport with anyone as long as you approach them from the mindset of offering them something they would find valuable. Give it some real thought and come up with a few things you can do for the person you're looking to influence this month. Make sure whatever you offer benefits them.

The Link Between Your Self-esteem and Connecting with Others

What is self-esteem, and how do you measure it? See if you can answer this question: On a scale of 1 to 10 (1=don't agree, 10=totally agree), how much do you agree with this statement, "I like myself just the way I am."

A high score isn't about pride or comparison. It's about self-acceptance, calmness, humility, gratitude, and generosity. People with high self-esteem don't talk down to others because they don't feel superior or better than those they are trying to make a connection with. That makes the bond with the person you're trying to communicate with deeper because they feel equal in your presence.

If you struggle with low self-esteem, then it's likely that you'll have a tendency to be pessimistic, jealous, insecure, hostile, and fearful of rejection. All these things may impair your ability to communicate effectively, causing the person on the receiving end to misinterpret your words even when you have the best intention. Inferiority and superiority complexes come about as a result of low self-esteem. One more thing I've learned about self-confidence is that it directly impacts how much courage and vulnerability an individual has. The more you work on your self-esteem, the easier it will be for you to embrace and even cope with uncomfortable situations. Instead of suppressing your vulnerability, you openly share it, and that creates an open space for sharing and connecting.

Therefore, when it comes to self-esteem, self-confidence, and developing deeper trust with others, the responsibility lies more on us than it does on the person we are interacting with.

Chapter 11: Show Them You're Really Listening

"The most important thing in communication is to hear what isn't being said." — Peter Drucker

It's important to recognize that everyone's feelings are valid. As you learn techniques to make you a better communicator, you should also develop ways of demonstrating to others that you're present and listening attentively. That will provide those around you a sense of comfort and understanding, even if it's during a trivial conversation. But how do you do this? The secret lies in being fully present and knowing when to maintain silence and when to speak. The more attentive, warm, open, and relaxed you are, the more the speaker will feel your presence. Let's discuss a few tips that will help you demonstrate that you are fully present and attentive.

How to Make Others Feel That You're Listening

• Ask open-ended questions

This is something you should always do in every conversation. Whether you're speaking with a co-worker, neighbor, or significant other, shift from simply nodding and passively listening and start being more interactive. Ask them things like "How is this impacting you?" or "Is there anything I can do for you right now?" Asking these types of questions will let the person know that you are listening and invested in their well-being.

• Become mindful of your body movement

If you often get nervous communicating with others or if you're not sure what kind of signals your body is sending out as you listen to others, ask a trusted friend for some feedback. Most of the time, we make funny faces, fiddle with our hair, jewelry, or clothing, or we keep shaking one leg, and all these things get picked up by the speaker. Some might interpret it as nervousness, but others might assume you're impatient, bored, or uninterested. Try to relax when someone else is speaking and you're silent. Take deep breaths and center yourself. If you catch your mind wandering or your leg shaking, that's okay; just stop and consciously bring yourself back into the present moment.

• Keep your phone away from the table

Whenever you sit to have a chat with someone, avoid the common habit that I see everywhere of placing your cellphone right next to you. I was recently watching a couple that came and sat next to me at a Starbucks coffee shop. What caught my attention was the fact that the guy had two cellphones on the table side by side, and the girl kept reaching into her handbag (on her lap) every few minutes to check her phone. It's easy to see why relationships are having so many communication issues. If you think the cellphone isn't a huge distraction, think again! Research shows it is, in fact, the enemy of presence, and it robs you of your power of attentive focus. So, if you actually wish to create a meaningful connection with someone, put the phone away, give them your full attention, and let the phone vibrate. I'm sure those text messages or notifications can wait a while.

When to Be Still and Silent

When it comes to being silent, practice makes perfect. Sometimes, the best way to show someone that you are listening is to be silent. If you recall the story of Dave and Shelly, Dave was able to show Shelly that he was listening to her by simply being still and allowing her to vent. There are situations when you will need to take a step back and let the passionate speaker have their way. This can be particularly helpful if you're the one in charge of others. When they come to you, especially with troubling news, before you start thinking about a solution, sit in silence and give them the gift of your presence.

Many husbands with great marriages can share the powerful impact of being silent. When the wife comes up and says to her husband, "I had the worst day ever. My friend did XYZ to me and caused me to end up late and derailed, and I had to skip my lunch which made me extra cranky all day..." The best thing that the husband can do is to sit back, take deep breaths, remain calm, open, warm, and attentive to his wife because she didn't come in need of a solution. She came to him because she wanted to feel heard, understood, and cared for. By practicing silence and maintaining warm, open body gestures and facial expressions that convey empathy, that wife will vent and move on. And she'll be glad she has a husband who "gets her."

Chapter 12: Persuasion or Empathy?

"Empathy is the capacity to think and feel oneself into the inner life of another person." — Heinz Kohut

In recent years I've become increasingly interested in the topic of persuasion mainly because I used to suck at it. I've studied this subject, interviewed some of the best experts, and even investigated the most persuasive people I have ever known. What I've learned came as a shock to me, and I hope it will delight and surprise you as well. Persuasion done genuinely isn't at odds with empathy. In fact, as it turns out, empathy is the ultimate persuasion tool.

The more empathy you can demonstrate as you communicate with others, the more likely your words will sink into them and drive the desired action. You see, in order to genuinely persuade someone, there must be an understanding of where they are. Persuasion is about moving someone from point A (their current standpoint on a subject matter) to point B (your desired standpoint on the same subject matter). You won't succeed in doing so if you don't even know their current starting point. Therefore, you need to gain an understanding of their point of view. For example, if you say, "You should join me because of our shared identity as Germans," and you aren't German, then that argument will fall flat. But if your

German heritage is significant to you and you are both of German origin, this argument would be highly persuasive.

Most of us struggle to get through to others because we assume that the person we are talking to is just like us or should be just like us. So, in this case, instead of finding a real common ground where both unique aspects are respected, a conflict would likely arise because the listener will feel unheard and undervalued. It's therefore mandatory that you raise your level of empathy and invest time figuring out what the right starting point is for the person you wish to persuade. That includes getting to understand a person's point of view and pain.

Understanding People's Pain

A famous story is often recounted of two skeptics who attended a new age healing seminar. They decided the workshop was unscientific and laughable. During a Q&A session with the organizers, one attendee asked if the healing process they were selling would cure insomnia. The organizer said it would. Another asked if it would help her stay awake longer as she was setting up a new digital business after putting her infant to sleep. The organizer said it would.

At this point, the skeptics had had enough. They stood up and pointed out that it was impossible for the same process to help someone both stay awake and fall asleep faster. They proceeded to debunk the organizer's claims. During the lunch break, they went around networking to find out if the attendees were ready to quit the ridiculous seminar. To their dismay, none had changed their mind. When the skeptics inquired why they would still sign up when the facts clearly demonstrated proved the whole thing absurd, each attendee simply said a version of "I'm struggling with this problem and what I need is a solution. This healing technique might just work! Your facts don't help me in any way!"

While the skeptics' arguments were valid, they didn't provide real solutions to the problems. These people were in real pain and what they needed was someone who understood them and offered a practical solution. The skeptics, lacking empathy and unable to consider the audience's pain, failed to use logic to persuade a different action.

Many times, we fail to persuade because empathy is missing. We might use the best words, fill our statement with facts and truth, and it might still not impact the other person or drive them to action because at the end of the day, people listen and follow someone they know, like, and trust. Empathy plays a significant role in building trust.

Don't Confuse Persuasion with Manipulation

Most people associate persuasion with manipulation. That is a grievous mistake. As a speaker, you want to influence and build rapport out of empathy, not manipulation or deception. Most people sell manipulation as the tool to "get people to listen and do what you want." However, this approach is rooted in insecurity, low self-esteem, and selfishness. In the end, it never works out. A selfish attitude centered on "what's in it for me" will always culminate in disaster. It is the opposite of genuine persuasion. The real question you should always be asking is, "What does the other person want and need, and is there a way for both of us to have what we want?"

A question I often get is, "Are you asking me to neglect my needs?" That's not what I'm suggesting here. Instead, I am recommending approaching this person from a higher perspective. If you have unmet needs urging you to reach out to this person (for example, you need to make a sale fast for financial reasons), you must work on your success mindset and coach yourself into serving first. Have awareness for your needs and show yourself compassion but recognize that understanding the other person and doing everything you can to empathize with them will make for more impactful communication than being focused on your unmet needs.

You Must Cast Pride Aside

One of the greatest hindrances to successful communication is pride. Most of us are driven by the ego in all our daily conversations. That makes it hard to effectively influence, persuade, and develop trust with the people who don't think or agree with you. Ego is also the main reason many people don't open themselves up to develop empathy. The moment you realize that your truth and the narrative you are telling yourself is equally as valuable as what the other person believes and says, a shift will happen within you. It's not about agreeing with their beliefs but about respecting their perspective.

Some people will read this book and still refuse to let go of their ego because it feels better to entertain that feeling of superiority. If you like to think of yourself as better than others (you employees, your colleagues, etc.), this one will require a lot of effort. You can read all the communication books you want, but it's going to be tough developing the kind of rapport you want with people. If you recognize that your pride gets in the way of genuinely understanding and connecting with others, it's a great opportunity to practice empathy.

When it comes to the other tools for persuasion, Robert Cialdini's books are great resources. But as I said, start with improving your empathy. Only then will you notice a shift in how people perceive and receive your words.

Chapter 13: Why Trust Matters

"I trust you is a better compliment than I love you because you do not always trust the person you love, but you can always love the person you trust." — *Anonymous*

What's hard to build, easy to destroy, and absolutely essential to any healthy relationship? Trust.

One of the tenets of developing deep connections and building rapport with others is trust. Trust plays a huge role in both our personal and professional relationships. It is fragile and really hard to fix once broken. That's why it's important to learn to protect that element of trust in a relationship as early on as possible. Taking measures to ensure the other person feels like you are trustworthy is something you can learn to facilitate. That's what this chapter will help you master. But first, a few examples of how trust issues emerge in our daily lives.

A mother struggles to give permission to her teenage son, who wants to attend a friend's birthday party over the weekend, because she doesn't trust him to resist the temptation of indulging in some bad habits. In a different city, a couple sits at a marriage counselor's office for the tenth time, still trying to work out their differences because, despite their love for each other, the wife doesn't feel like she can ever trust her husband. Why? He lied about his business trip and only confessed after she discovered it was a secret getaway with a fling. In both these scenarios, love is evident but trust is missing, and that makes all the difference. None of these relationships can truly flourish because they equally lack trust. Unless each individual in the relationship can feel like they fully trust the other person, a deep, genuine connection is impossible.

Social scientist and best-selling author Brené Brown says, "Trust is built in very small moments." That means the daily or simple things you do as you interact with a person. Instead of going for grand gestures, reach for small, consistent efforts that you can regularly do for the other person.

For example, when a teenager lies over simple things like who is texting or what they were watching, unknowing to them is that their parents start to lose that respect needed to allow them more of the freedom they want. The same is true in adult relationships. But sometimes, in adult relationships, it's even more complex than that. For example, if you're in bed reading a book and the urge to pee strikes, you put the book aside for a few minutes and excitedly dash to the bathroom. On your way back, you notice your spouse on the other side of the room looking troubled. Now you have two options. You can either ignore their sad look and jump back into your book or forgo the reading and go talk to your spouse to find out why they seem so troubled. Being attuned to your partner in that way and responding to their emotions sends a signal that you understand and empathize with them, which helps develop trust.

Keys to Developing Trust

There are elements vital for trust-building, the most fundamental being respect, effective communication, vulnerability, transparency, and reliability. Let's take a look at each.

Respect
While this may sound obvious, respect is key to establishing trust with others. Your tone, how you refer to others, and how you treat them will determine whether people trust you or not. If the other person doesn't feel like you have genuine respect for them, whether it's a personal or professional relationship, things will fall apart. I know this one might prove difficult for some, especially if you tend to come off as arrogant or condescending, but it's high time to make some shifts. That is one of the key aspects I had to adjust in myself because my tone would often come across as demeaning, which resulted in tension and lack of trust.

Effective Communication
Instead of just the general talk about communication that we've covered throughout this book, let's get a little more nuanced and share ways to improve your communication, especially in tough situations. The first thing you should do when you notice your emotions flare-up is to keep yourself in check. If anger creeps in, stop and set some boundaries with those who anger you. It will prevent you from putting out words and actions to match those internal feelings. Give yourself some buffer time to acknowledge the emotion and also question what will happen if you lose control. A good

statement to complete is, "If I lose control... [state the consequence of acting out]." It's not about being right. It's about reaching the ultimate goal that you most desire and ensuring that your actions don't become a hindrance.

You can also increase the amount of "listening" time you invest in your relationships. The more you integrate the strategies you've learned in this book, such as being present, empathetic, and mindful, the easier it will be to increase your capacity to listen. As you listen, you'll get to hear anxieties, fears, and even read between the lines making it easier for you to build rapport and ultimately get what you want out of the relationship.

Vulnerability
Our society has shamed the idea of being open and vulnerable, making it seem like a weakness. The truth is only truly brave and strong individuals are capable of being vulnerable. So, if you think it makes you weak, think again!

Now I know you might be wondering, "But what if I come across as an incompetent person or what if it backfires on me?" The best way to approach this concern is to realize that vulnerability always includes having boundaries and being conscious of the situation and context one is in. That helps you avoid oversharing or giving away too much. So, if you're sharing your emotions or experiences in the workplace, then they should be in some way relevant to that environment so that out of that sharing, those involved feel more connected. It should be something that moves your work and relationship forward.

We always need to investigate our intention for sharing and always question what we want to share, who we are sharing with, and whether it's relevant and right for us to do so.

Just because we talk about sharing your feelings, being authentic, and speaking your truth doesn't mean you should share everything with all people at all times. Let me give you an illustration of this. Suppose you're in charge of a start-up and things are going awry. You have a meeting with investors coming up soon, and your quarterly staff meeting is in 24 hours. So far, you have nothing but grim news to share with everyone. The company is bleeding. You feel like you're in over your head, and you have no way out of the current mess. What do you think is the next best step? What would be a demonstration of vulnerability in such a case?

I've asked this question in several of my masterminds, and usually, people say the right thing is to tell the truth to the employees and investors that there's no hope. They seem to see this as being vulnerable and authentic. But this is a far cry from what it means to be vulnerable. It's a good idea to tell someone about the current crisis and ask for help dealing with this challenge, but who is the right person to have that conversation with? I can assure you, telling your employees and investors you don't know what you're doing will only lead to more failure. You will never get anyone to fund your ideas again, and you'll instill a sense of fear and financial pressure on every great employee you have who left a perfectly good job to come and support your dream. Is that really who you are?

So, think back to your life and the current relationships you have, both personal and professional. Are there ways you can show up more authentically and vulnerable without compromising your values and personality? If you're not the sharing kind and you love your privacy, you can still be vulnerable by simply letting others know when you're having an off day. If it's an intimate relationship and you don't like sharing your work with your spouse, simply let them know that you're struggling with something at work. It's hard, but you're figuring it out, and you just wanted them to know that you're not in a bad mood or distancing yourself. You simply need a little time to gain clarity and solve this issue. Tell them what support looks like for you. Perhaps it's giving you some extra quiet time for you to be with your thoughts. Tell your spouse what you need right now and what feels right for you. You can apply this to any relationship, and I can assure you the person on the receiving end will appreciate your openness even though you didn't necessarily disclose your emotions.

Transparency

The simplest description I can offer of transparency is operating in a way that creates openness between you and those you're interacting with. That can be with your intimate relations or at work. This type of openness creates trust and leads to successful outcomes for all parties. But you should know that transparency is an ongoing process, and qualities like honesty, effective communication, empathy, and vulnerability all work together to build on transparency.

Being transparent isn't about being a jerk or harming others with your words, truthful as they might be. Let me ask you this: have you experienced one of those bosses who calls an employee a "lazy good-for-nothing" and justifies it by saying it's a fact based on lack of results or failed projects? I have. And it didn't feel good at all even though the remark wasn't addressed to me. Speaking our truth can be done in a manner that doesn't demean another human being. And when we learn to be transparent, we develop the skill of speaking our truth in an authentic, kind, and human-focused way.

Reliability

When it comes to your relationships, you want to be the person others feel they can trust right from the get-go. There are different ways to express trust, including:
• Listening, understanding, and supporting the other person
• Being thoughtful of the other person's needs
• Approaching conflict in a healthy and mature way
• Creating a safe space
• Doing your best not to overreact or judge harshly before knowing all the facts
• Respecting personal boundaries
• Not being dominating or controlling
• Matching your words with actions
• Being authentic

How Can You Start Building Trust in Your Relationships?

#1: Always be honest and authentic

Speaking your truth with empathy will always outshine and out win any clever quips or charming scripts you could come up with. In both personal and professional relationships, you want your message to convey the truth.

#2: Don't hide your feelings

Emotions are not a sign of weakness. And being open and vulnerable is a good thing in a relationship. If you struggle with this, I encourage you to check out Brené Brown's books. Showing people that you care is part of emotional intelligence, so acknowledge your feelings and use them to your advantage. Don't let them use you, however.

#3: Keep your word and follow through with actions

The purpose of building trust is to have others believe in you and what you say. Therefore, you not only need to think carefully about your words and the promises you make, but you should also see things through when you say you will. Keeping your word shows others what you expect from them, and in turn, you're more likely to receive the same treatment. You might hear a lot of people complain that people never treat them with respect. A little observation might just reveal that the same complainers often make promises they don't keep, or they keep saying things they don't mean. These small behaviors often trigger a lack of respect from others. If you want people to respect you, show them that you operate from a place of integrity.

#4: Practice patience

Building trust is an ongoing process. You can't just take one huge leap and be done with it. It's about small incremental steps taken consistently as you work on the relationship. Trust also takes time to develop because the more your actions demonstrate that you're trustworthy, the easier it will be to earn their trust. So be patient and stay committed. Every effort will pay off in the long run.

Chapter 14: Building a Deeper Connection

"I define connection as the energy that exists between people when they feel seen, heard, and valued; when they can give and receive without judgment; and when they derive sustenance and strength from the relationship." — Brené Brown

Our society has never been more technologically connected, and yet the cry for connection still ensues. Forty-seven percent of Americans describe feeling disconnected, solitary, or isolated, and a third of adults suffer from chronic loneliness. In fact, did you know that the World Health Organization declared loneliness a public health concern a while back? And that was even before the 2019/20 pandemic hit. To say that we all need to learn to develop deeper connections is an understatement. And I'm not talking about the brief, shallow encounters you have with so-called friends who are really acquaintances, co-workers, services people, social media followers, classmates, etc. I am talking about really investing in developing true friendships that are deep and enriching.

We Are Hard-wired for Connection

Humans are social creatures. We rely on each other for a sense of belonging, identity, validation, acceptance, love, and so much more. Feeling a sense of connection with another is vital if you want to enjoy a thriving relationship.

There's an ongoing Harvard Study of Adult Development. It is the longest in recorded history spanning 80 years thus far, and the results they're sharing surprise everyone, including me. "Close relationships, more than money or fame, are what keep people happy throughout their lives. Those ties protect people from life's discontents, help to delay mental and physical decline, and are better predictors of long and happy lives than social class, IQ, or even genes." — as reported by Liz Meneo in *The Harvard Gazette*.

Would you like to lead a long, happy, and fulfilling life? It turns out the secret lies in developing close connections. The biggest and best lessons you will ever have are found in your connections with others. Your best opportunities and gifts are also found in your relationships, both personal and professional. Although relationships require work, they also provide the best rewards. That's why you need to invest time deepening your relationships with friends, family, peers, co-workers, clients, and partners.

Discard Superficial Connectedness

There is a lot of fake connectedness going around. Perhaps social media has amplified an already existing problem, and that has made it more apparent, but too many of us practice avoidance and settle for superficial interactions. There's no depth to the conversations we have anymore. Small has become the only talk. Why is that? Are we suffering from chronic avoidance behavior? Is it really better to suppress your feelings just because you're scared to feel the discomfort of confrontation or sharing something vulnerable?

If we want meaningful connections that matter, we need to engage in meaningful conversations, including asking meaningful questions and allowing ourselves to be vulnerable.

It often feels safe and more comfortable to talk about the weather or last week's game, but if you want to develop a connection with someone, you need to take a risk and push the conversation in a new direction. That's the only way to learn something interesting about them. But you should never be pushy or creepy about it. Don't just jump into a conversation with a prospect and immediately ask about their deep and personal lives right away. Obviously, you can inquire about their family, values, hobbies, etc., when it is appropriate, so you need to learn the art of timing.

The same is true when you're talking to someone senior or junior to you in the workplace. Asking deeply personal questions is great, but only when appropriate and well-phrased. Here are a few meaningful questions to help inspire you. My challenge to you now is to pick just one and ask the next person you'll engage in a conversation with. The more you practice this, the better you will become.

#1: What does your ideal/perfect day look like for you?
#2: Name three things you and your partner appear to have in common.
#3: What do you currently feel most grateful for in your life?
#4: If you could change anything in your life about the way you were raised, what would it be?

#5: Is there something you've dreamed about doing for a long time now? Why haven't you done it?
#6: What do you value most in a friendship?
#7: When did you last cry in front of another person? When did you last do it by yourself?
#8: How close and warm is your family? Do you feel your childhood was happier than most other people's?
#9: Do you think it's okay to be vulnerable in relationships?
#10: What is the greatest accomplishment of your life?

How to Start Building Deeper Connections

Reflect for a moment on how connected you feel to your family, current relationships at work, and friends. How much depth do these relationships have? If you realize some work is needed and you'd like to improve, this chapter shares simple things you can start doing to build stronger and deeper connections.

• Create an emotional space where people feel comfortable enough to open up

Arthur Aron conducted a study that inevitably showed that people feel closer and more connected when they share intimate stories. Of course, how intimate the story is depends largely on the context of the relationship and the current situation. But sharing something human and personal is always a good idea, especially if it's relevant to the other person. So how would you go about encouraging people to open up to you? The best way to get someone to drop their mask is to make them feel comfortable. Start by asking deep questions as if it were the most normal thing in the world. When the person answers, listen without judgment. Nod and make them feel heard and understood. When they finish, share your own story or something similar that would enhance that resonance. It really is that simple, but of course, depending on the situation, you might require a little creativity. For example, if you're with someone who doesn't want to open up.

When you notice someone pushing back on your questions, don't get frazzled or shift your energy. Remain calm and try to ease them into it by answering the question first so they can see there's nothing wrong with the topic. If they still don't open up, perhaps it might be the case that you're not yet comfortable with doing this yourself, and you're projecting mixed signals which might put them off. It will take a while for you to get the hang of being this emotionally astute, so when things backfire, don't panic. Simply take a step back into regular chit chat and try again later.

- Listen with your heart

Become more aware of how you listen to others. Think about the five people in your life you spend the most time with. Do you usually hear them speak and immediately engage in internal dialogue prepping yourself for a response? Do you have a tendency to finish their sentences or interrupt them with your own experiences? Are you listening to your inner dialogue and making assumptions or judgments about the other person?

Listening from your heart brings you to the present moment, engages both your head and emotions, and unconsciously sends out signals that the other picks up. And that makes them feel genuinely heard. When that happens, it deepens your level of trust and connection with them.

- Dig deeper

This is about continuing your own inner work and personal growth. The more you work on understanding yourself, uncovering old patterns, limiting beliefs, and false perceptions about people, the more your perspective shifts. How you approach and relate to people also changes, and that positively impacts all your interactions. As your journey unfolds, you realize that everyone in your life plays a significant role in your life experience, and you start to appreciate that.

As you come to this realization, you inevitably see that just as you're on your journey of becoming better and increasing awareness, so too is everyone else. That imbues you with a sense of calm, compassion, and understanding that makes interacting with others very enjoyable. Certain things that would tick you off in the past no longer hold you captive, and you are able to rise to any challenging situation with a lot more emotional maturity. People love being around emotionally mature individuals. They also tend to trust those that demonstrate this level of mental and spiritual maturity.

- Be present and focused on the other person

Many of us don't realize this, but hardly anyone invests as much time thinking about us as we like to assume! Everyone is too busy thinking about themselves and their issues. So, when you take things personally or forget to shift your focused attention from yourself to the person interacting with you, it's hard to create a deep connection with that other person.

Here's what you need to do: whenever you're interacting with a human being, set aside your selfish needs and thoughts and be entirely focused on them. Yes, that includes a prospect or client. Ask about their lives, families, hobbies, goals, and visions. Then incorporate the first tip and "listen with your heart." Invest that time relating with them through your body language, facial expression, and overall quality of presence. Be there with them at that moment. Do not check your phone notifications or people passing by you or sitting across the table. Be mindful and allow no distractions. Do not engage in the mental judgment of the other person. Simply be there for them with your full attention. Notice the difference it makes in the quality of your connection.

• Alternate depth with humor

You've heard it said, laughter is the best medicine. It's also a great technique for creating an instant connection with anyone as long as you do it appropriately. Laughter releases oxytocin, and even more importantly, it says you share similar personalities.

So, I recommend combining these two. Ask those deep questions, go deep, and then balance it out with some laughter. If you only talk about deep serious or personal issues, you run the risk of coming across as too invasive or suffocating. Most people will eventually feel a disconnect with you, so what you should do is approach it more like a freediving experience. Sometimes you must come up for air before going deep again.

- Actively give love

Relationships are always an act of giving before receiving. When you actively give love, it becomes a practical state that the other person can experience at that moment. Get into the habit of doing things for and with people that demonstrate that you love them. Both personal and professional relationships can improve considerably when you express that you care.

Make someone laugh at work, offer them a coffee or a helping hand. If it's a client, give them an extra service or solve a problem for them at no additional charge. Give a foot rub to your loved one or surprise them with a nourishing meal when they come home on a Friday night. If a friend or relative is having a tough time, be there for them and allow them to cry on your shoulder. These are all loving gestures, and they are far more powerful than any purchased gift. They all express, "I care for your well-being," and that is invaluable for any human being. How you make others feel (especially if they feel loved) will go a long way in establishing trust. As Maya Angelou once said, "People will forget what you said, people will forget what you did, but people will never forget how you made them feel."

- Build an "Us vs. the World" experience

If you can find a way to "poke fun at the world" with the person you want to build a connection with, it'll go a long way in establishing that feeling of trust. I have seen this work in both personal and professional relationships. For example, if you're in sales and a prospect walks in, but you create an environment where he feels like you're working for him instead of working for the company, you're more likely to get the man's business. I experienced this with a real estate agent a few years back. She worked for a big real estate firm, and every house she took me to, as she helped me negotiate the rent, I felt she didn't even care about her commission or how much the owner would make. She used words and made proposals that leaned more on getting me the best deal. I immediately dropped all my other agents and eventually settled for a house that she recommended. That's the power of "us vs. the world" in the context of relationship building.

Chapter 15: Techniques for Listening with Intention

"We think we listen, but very rarely do we listen with real understanding and true empathy. Yet listening of this very special kind is one of the most potent forces for change that I know."
— Carl Rogers.

For most of us reading this book, we've come to the most practical section where we invest time consciously learning and hopefully integrating the strategies discussed here because the only way to build rapport and become a master communicator is to excel at listening. If by now you realize that you naturally struggle to actively listen, demonstrate empathy, or simply be present with another, you're not alone. It does take conscious effort at first. We've all had to put in the time and practice. But it does get easier, and the results are worthwhile. Remember, active listening isn't just a matter of gathering information. It's also about gaining perspective and understanding. So, let's talk about my top five techniques.

Technique #1: Smile
Yes, it is that simple. A smile is powerful when interacting with a human being. Smiling has been scientifically shown to lower stress and improve your mood in the process. And not only that, but smiling is also pretty contagious. Our brains are hard-

wired to notice and interpret other people's facial expressions automatically and, more often than not, mimic them.

That means when you interact with someone, one of you will influence the other's mood and body language. By training yourself to communicate with others while holding a genuine smile, the other person will feel an elevation of mood as their brain picks up on your happy state. There's also plenty of research that suggests that smiling causes us to appear more successful and confident. When in a professional setting, either trying to vie for a promotion or perhaps a job interview or closing a client, this will help you come across as the best person for the deal. Even if you're trying to get a date, asking someone out with a smile on your face (not a creepy fake one) is more likely to get you a yes.

Technique #2: Allow silence
Most people get nervous when there's silence during a conversation. Yes, it can feel awkward and strange, but a pause allows the speaker and listener time to soak in what's been said. It enables the people engaging in conversation to gather their thoughts and respond accordingly instead of reacting. Silence has a real purpose in our conversations. Often we associate people who can't seem to shut up as being nervous and people who are good at being silent and taking long pauses in between conversations as calm and confident.

The idea that silence is awkward is really just a matter of perception. If you signal confidence, silence is just silence. And what I've learned is that the deeper the conversation, the more silence is appreciated. It almost acts as a bonding moment for the people engaged. Think of some of the best pieces of music you've ever listened to. Notice how they all make very good use of silence. They pause and use silence as a technique for creating a more emotional attachment and dramatic effect. You can do something similar using silence. Whether it's with a casual friend, an intimate partner, or a client that you're trying to close, try using a few seconds of silence every now and then. Notice how drawn they become to your every word. It's almost as though they want to listen to you more.

Technique #3: Avoid interrupting
Whether it's a phone call, a team meeting, or arguing with your spouse, interrupting someone as they speak is a bad habit to get into. It tells the person that you don't care about their opinion or what they have to say. In many ways, it's a show of disrespect which makes it hard for the other person to listen or take action on your instructions.

So, what should you do? Be silent and wait until there's a natural break in the conversation. When it's a very sensitive or heated conversation, you could consider saying, "I have some thoughts if you'd be open to hearing them," or "Can I follow up with a question?" This makes sure that the interaction remains a conversation that is positive and encouraged by all parties. If you tend to interrupt people because an idea came to mind and you don't want to lose it, here are a few more hacks for you.

• Carry a small notebook and jot down those thoughts as they come.

• Hold off on the questions and keep your focus on the person. If you allow your brain to wander off and formulate responses and questions while the other person is still speaking, you're more likely to interrupt because you're no longer present. Stay focused on the person in front of you. Don't interrogate. Be present and maintain eye contact.

Technique #4: P.A.C.E. the conversation
This is a simple formula that many powerful communicators use. The P.A.C.E. acronym stands for Purpose, Ask, Connect, and Encourage.

Purpose: When speaking with someone, you want to determine the purpose of that conversation and your intended message, especially if you're the one delivering some important information. Make sure that is clear even before you initiate conversation.

Ask: You need to ask a relevant, thoughtful, high-quality question to make sure the other person feels engaged. Always respond with a question so you can dig deeper, gain more context, and understand the other person's point of view. This is also a great way to reconfirm that the other person actually got what you intended them to understand. If you're giving a briefing at work, then you might want to end with something like "Does that make sense to you?" or "Would you like to repeat back what you got?"

If it's an intimate relationship, you could ask, "What did you understand from this honey?" If you're part of the conversation and you just heard something that wasn't clear, then perhaps a better response would be, "Can you tell me what you mean by that?"

Connect: This is about observing body language. Become mindful about what signals your body is giving off to ensure you're not repelling the other person or sending mixed signals. The same is true if you're listening to the person. You want to make sure what the person is saying, and the nonverbal cues are a match.

For example, I can recall a staff meeting where my boss walked us through very technical analysis and then asked my colleague to put together a briefing that summarized everything he just said. My colleague verbally responded, "Yes, boss," but the glazed look on her face and the strange, defeated body posture demonstrated she didn't have a clue what she was doing. Later that day, I found her wallowing at her desk, and I asked, "Do you need help with that briefing document?" She was astonished! She couldn't figure out how I had known she had no idea what was expected of her. But anyone mindful and aware enough of body language could have seen it right there and then.

Encourage: This is about building positive reinforcement and acknowledging people's strengths. If the person you're talking to feels like you value and appreciate their input, they are more likely to do what you want them to do. A friend once told me that she gets her teenage boys to clean their rooms each week and make their beds every morning before school simply because of how much praise and appreciation she offers them. "I make it a big deal in my house. I'm always talking to all my neighbors about how clean and thoughtful my teenage boys are and how lucky I am to have them. The boys love hearing other people speak highly of them around the neighborhood, so they keep living up to that as much as possible." Your client, friend, boss, employee, colleague, or spouse will likely have the same positive response when you genuinely encourage and praise them whenever possible.

Technique #5: Learn to paraphrase and restate things

I took a MasterClass with Chris Voss, a famous negotiator and retired FBI hostage negotiator, who made me realize the importance of restating and paraphrasing. It's a technique that he used to handle some pretty sticky and potentially fatal situations. Given how successful he has been using this technique, it's only natural I recommend it to you.

When you paraphrase, be sure not to repeat word for word because you risk sounding like a copycat. That's very annoying! Instead, you should attempt to say it back to them, emphasizing the emotion you picked up on so that they can clarify whether or not you're on the same page. If the feeling or words you chose don't quite resonate with the person, they will likely correct you, which is what you want in this case. For example, if someone says to you, "I am just extremely vexed by this, and I'm not sure how to fix it." You would paraphrase or restate that along the lines of "So what I hear you say is that this thing is frustrating you, and you're trying to figure out how to solve it?"

Chapter 16: How to Give People Space and Still Show That You Care

"Sometimes giving someone space is the most selfless thing you can do." — *Brownell Landrum*

Being a great communicator and developing deep personal relationships includes what goes unspoken. Learning to create a safe space for others to "just be" is a skill anyone can learn. Creating space in your relationship might seem counterintuitive. For example, you have a fight with your child or spouse, and the last thing you want is for them to walk away. The same is true if things go wrong with your boss or an unhappy client. Most people want to talk more and stay in the same room until things get resolved. Sometimes, that's not the best solution if you wish to preserve your relationship.

Has anyone you care about ever asked you for some space? I bet your stomach tightened immediately and you felt anxious. That negative buildup is often unnecessary. It comes from social conditioning we all have where we assume time apart is a bad thing.

The truth is, having a thriving relationship is about knowing when to spend time in person talking a lot and when to give each other space. So, the first thing you need to do is shift your perspective. Once you recognize that the moment requires some silence and distance, let the other person know that you respect them enough to give them space. Let them know you are ready to pick things up and continue with your discussion when they feel ready. Here are a few other pointers:

• Make it a positive experience through your attitude

Your attitude will determine how the other person perceives this gesture. If you're sulking and using an insecure and negative tone, it's unlikely this will help the other person open up soon. Instead of making it seem like you're being punished or that they are wrong, focus on making them feel okay for wanting this space. Use positive language. You could say something like, "I understand you need some space to clear your mind. I will be here whenever you need me."

• Communicate a plan

Another way to show you care and a better response when someone won't communicate with you when you want is by being clear about when you would like to reconnect. That way, you both know what to expect, and it becomes a little easier to deal with that "time off." That is especially beneficial in a work situation. If you and a colleague cannot see eye to eye, but you know you must resolve it, a better approach would be to ask them when they would be ready to have a meeting and find an amicable solution. They might say, "Give me three days," at which point you can accept and paraphrase back the agreed-upon date and time for your discussion.

One of the couples we like to do date night with uses a similar technique when they get into an argument. The husband is usually very calm and slow to temper. His wife is a bit short-tempered. Whenever they disagree, he just wants to walk out of the house to cool off, and she wants to keep raising her voice till it's fixed. They came up with an agreed plan that whenever things get rough, he will get up and ask for his space, and she will allow it on the condition that he tells her when they will finish the conversation. Usually, it's a date within 24 hours of the disagreement. They say it has improved their communication tremendously.

Chapter 17: Words That Build Trust in Any Relationship

"Sticks and stones can break my bones, but words can never hurt me." — Unknown

Although that saying is pretty common, it's also completely false. Words can build or tear down a relationship. It's important to remember that the way you perceive trust might differ from how others perceive it. That's why you need to combine your word choice with an outward expression of respect.

Words are powerful, and they do matter. They build a psychological connection between people and profoundly impact us all. When that's followed up with the right behavior, you have a greater impact on the person listening to you speak. Notice how well you demonstrate that you respect the person you're talking to through tone of voice, body language, and so on. The words you chose and the impressions, images, and expectations you create through your words will influence your relationships. At work, with family, friends, neighbors, and strangers, you can inspire, deflate, diminish, or enable the listener. We've shared many hacks around effective communication. Still, I wanted to share real-world examples of words that cause harm and words that build rapport so you can start creating a personal dictionary for your interactions.

Trust Diminishing Words

Do you know what words can cause someone to distrust you instantly? Call someone an idiot or blockhead at work, and you won't get very far with them. Call someone a drama king or queen, and tension immediately rises. Other examples of trust diminishing words:
a. Do as I say, not as I do.
b. That's stupid because...
c. It's not my fault because...
d. You should have known better.

Notice how in all these examples, there's a lack of responsibility and a lot of fault finding and negative labeling on your end.

Examples of words that build trust:
a. I understand what you're saying.
b. In my opinion...
c. How do you think you performed?
d. What can I do differently next time?
e. I am all ears.
f. That was my fault.
g. What can I do to help?

In contrast to the earlier examples, notice how these statements take responsibility, demonstrate empathy, and offer a helping/supporting hand. The lesson here is that using words that empower and enable can help you establish a strong rapport and promote trust with another.

Tips for Giving Feedback Without Destroying Trust

Giving constructive feedback is often hard for many of us. It's uncomfortable and requires a particular skill set that many don't acquire. Since you will need to give and get feedback, it's important to address that aspect of communication. When you want to give feedback without damaging your reputation or the trust you've built, the best approach is to consider yourself more like a coach than a disciplinarian.

#1: Be direct and candid.
That doesn't mean you should be harsh or unkind. Instead, you can say, "What I'm observing is..." or "I couldn't help but notice that..."

#2: Be empathetic and vulnerable.
Infusing empathy and some vulnerability into the conversation will cause the listener to receive the news better. You could even say, "This is awkward for me to say, but I need to do it..." or "This isn't easy for me, [name]; however, I want us to talk openly about..."

Validation Responses

It is important to learn emotional validation when communicating with others because it fosters acceptance, strengthens your relationship, shows that you value the other person, and leads to better emotional regulation for everyone concerned. Improving this skill can not only make you a better communicator, but it also teaches you how to validate your own thoughts and feelings. Let's talk about how you can begin today.

- Identify and acknowledge the emotion

The first thing you must learn to do is acknowledge the emotion that the other is experiencing. I know this is hard to do at first, especially if you're dealing with someone who isn't good at expressing their true feelings or someone overly aggressive. Still, with a bit of practice, you can develop enough self-control and emotional mastery to hold a safe space for them even when it feels uncomfortable for you.

For example, imagine that a loved one is angry with you for reasons you don't quite get. You come home one evening from work and notice the cold treatment and snarky remarks. They may not explicitly say they are angry, but you can tell they are by the behavior. In this scenario, it might be best to give them time to state out loud what they are feeling, at which point you can acknowledge, "I understand you're feeling angry."

If they don't communicate directly that they are angry, a good option would be to open with a question like, "You seem angry. Is that what's going on?"

- Acknowledge the source of the emotion

The next step is to identify the situation that triggered the emotion. You might say something like, "What's making you feel this way?" Sometimes you might get a clear answer, but other times you won't, and that's okay.

- Validate the emotion

This is one of the most critical aspects of your communication. It's where you acknowledge the other person's feelings and hold that open space for them to express their emotions without being judged or shamed freely. Coming back to our example of realizing your loved one is angry; here's how you would respond to them. If your beloved says they are angry because you came home late and missed date night, you can still validate their feelings even if you don't think being angry is warranted. Especially when you know you haven't done anything wrong. So, this is where you'll take a deep breath and say, "I understand you're feeling angry because I missed date night. It was out of my control because the boss kept us all late working on a new account. It wasn't my intention to anger you, but I can see that waiting for me made you upset."

In other words, give your reason for being late and don't feel like you have to apologize for your actions if you didn't do anything wrong. Remember to make them aware that you respect their point of view as well.

More examples of validating responses:
- I can see how you would feel that way.
- That must be really hard.
- I bet you're frustrated.
- I'm here for you.
- I'm so happy for you! You've worked incredibly hard on this. It must feel amazing.
- You have every right to be proud; that's a major accomplishment.
- Ah, that is so sad.
- Wow, that would drive me crazy too!
- He really said that? I'd be angry too!

The bottom line is that you need to identify a specific emotion and offer justification for that emotion so that the other person feels accepted and understood by you. It's not about compromising your beliefs or agreeing with everything another says. Instead, it's about agreeing with the fact that they are right to feel as they do. The next time someone shares something with you, try validating them. It can be a fear, dream, experience, or anything else that expresses their emotion. Get into that same experience and identify the predominant emotion they are feeling or articulating, and show them that you understand and respect the way they are feeling.

Chapter 18: How to Read and Analyze People Better

"To know what people really think, pay regard to what they do, rather than what they say." — Rene Descartes

This book would not be complete without an in-depth discussion on emotions and how to read people better. By now, you must have realized that emotions impact behavior, attitudes, and in turn, communication. It doesn't matter how skilled you are as a communicator or how many techniques you've learned. If you're not good at reading emotions, you're still going to miss the mark.

Take the example of this story that a friend recounted. I asked her the reason for her recent break up with a man she was very fond of. A few months earlier, she was talking about marriage and settling down. Yet now, they were no longer together. This is what she said to me:

"Harry was everything I thought I wanted in a man. He's smart, successful, has strong values, and the kind of work ethic my parents would appreciate. Things were great the first six months, but there was an issue that kept growing worse. He simply never understood me. I would share something exciting about my day, and he would listen attentively, which I like. Still, his expressionless face and the fact that he would just respond with a single word were such a downer after engaging in conversation.

Last month I got a promotion at work. It's something I've been working on since before we started dating. As you can imagine, I couldn't wait to share my news with him. So, I planned a romantic dinner which went great. Then I told him I have big news to share. We sat on my front porch, and I began recounting my story with a lot of excitement, describing it very animatedly. He sat there unmoved with a plain (albeit pleasant) look on his face. Not once did he interrupt or participate in my action telling. Harry just sat there motionless. I might as well be talking to the flower pot on my porch. So finally, I was done, and I said: 'And finally the boss said, Sharon, the position is yours!' I literally shrieked in excitement at that moment. Harry was silent a minute too long if you ask me and then said, 'Wow, babe, that's really cool.'

That was it. I sank back and waited for him to say something more. He still maintained eye contact, and I think when we started feeling uncomfortable, he asked, 'What is it?'

I mean, are you kidding me? That's not someone I can have a conversation with or raise children together. He might be a nice boyfriend but certainly not a great husband, and since I'm looking for something serious, I figured it was best not to waste his time."

I've heard variations of this complaint many times with friends, colleagues, and relatives. The culprit, in this case, is the inability to read emotions and respond accordingly. Even if you're a great listener and speaker, you still need to read and analyze other people, and what their emotions are communicating so you can create that connection. Without that connection, everything else will fall flat.

This chapter will dive deep into the emotional scale and then share techniques you can use to read people so you can respond appropriately as you communicate with them.

The Emotional Scale

What is the dominant emotion through which you view life? And better still, are you able to quickly determine the emotional state of another as they receive your message? Knowing the filter someone is using to listen to you can help you adjust your tone, body language, and more as you speak to ensure the message gets through the way you intend and that it has a positive effect.

Some people filter everything through the emotional lens of apathy, fear, latent hostility, anger, pain, empathy, optimism, passion, and the list goes on and on. On the scale of emotions, we have states that range from the negative spectrum to the positive and everything in between. The further apart you and the listener are in your emotional states, the harder it will be to get your message across. For example, if you're speaking to someone who is really angry and you're passing on your message from a place of joy, it's unlikely you'll build rapport. Your body language, tone, and how you frame the news will create dissonance for the receiver, and they are likely to ignore or lash out even more. The same is true if you're communicating with someone who is in a joyful state of happiness. If you're stuck in apathy, the other person won't buy a word of it regardless of what you say. So how do you deal with this?

Increase your awareness of the most dominant emotions that ruin your day. The more aware you become of how you feel and how you behave due to those emotions, the easier it will be to spot others. Your intention should be to gain more control of how you feel so that you can lean in the direction of emotions that tend to attract a more positive interaction. Then you need to expand on this a little more and see if you can become more aware of how others feel. When you capture what another is conveying, call forth your empathy so that you can create a connection. You don't have to sympathize, force, and pretend to feel exactly as they do. Instead, you want to empathize so that you can understand how they must be feeling while still being true to your own emotions.

Coming back to the story about my friend and her boyfriend Harry—they could have salvaged that relationship if Harry had been more aware of his girlfriend's emotions. His lack of empathy and inability to read and understand her feelings was inevitably the giant wall that was built over time, making their communication impossible even though he was, in fact, a pretty good listener. You can avoid this same experience by emotional self-mastery and increasing your empathy and mindfulness so you can quickly identify what the other is feeling and respond accordingly.

6 Techniques for Reading People

#1 Start with a baseline
It's impossible to assume that one formula can make you a people-reading genius. We are all different with unique patterns of behavior and quirks. For example, some people might scratch their head, stroke their neck, squint, pout, or

jiggle their feet frequently. Others might cross their arms or legs, and none of it might be related to the stereotype ideas you read on the Internet. It could simply be a mannerism or a cultural side effect. However, there are always some signals that convey anger, deception, or nervousness. The only way to know whether someone is staring at the floor and avoiding eye contact out of respect or deception is to create a baseline for that individual. You need to figure out what "normal" behavior looks like for a person before you can identify their abnormal signals. For example, what emotions and body signals does the person convey when you talk about less trivial things like the weather or lunch with a friend?

I often give this advice to my single friends when they are interacting with someone new. Ask about the other person's social life to see how they change in emotional tone, body language, and energy. If you're having dinner with someone who struggles to say something pleasant about the food, their parents, best friend, or job, it's unlikely this is someone who will be radiating excitement when you're happy. It's also very unlikely they will feel connected with you if you're overly optimistic and love to praise and appreciate everything. A better form of communication and a lot more empathy is required for that dinner to go well.

#2 Notice the deviations

Once you've established the norm or baseline behavior, it's time to increase your mindfulness. Pay attention to the inconsistencies as you move through the conversation. Let's consider an example of a work conversation. Suppose you've created a baseline of your employee, and you've learned they usually clear their throat when they are nervous. If the person starts doing that while presenting the "small changes" they want to make to the approved budget, you might want to probe further. Ask a few more questions than you would typically to ensure you get to the heart of this inconsistency. Perhaps there's more here than meets the eye.

#3 Look for clusters of gestures
One thing we must clarify is that you can't read someone based on one gesture or word. You need to observe a series of behavioral aberrations, word choice, and emotional expressions to make an accurate conclusion. For example, your employee clearing her throat can also not mean she's hiding something, but simply clearing something out of her throat. But if her tone of voice, attitude, and behavior are off, she's not maintaining her usual eye contact, and she keeps shuffling her feet, then you have enough data to read. In that case, the clearing of the throat was one of several signals that alert you that you need to proceed with caution.

#4 Compare and contrast
If you're dealing with someone you already know well, like an employee or loved one, it can be a bit easier to compare and contrast with past behavior just by activating your memory. But suppose it's someone new and you're not sure how to read this situation. In that case, I would advise taking some time to allow the person to show more of themselves. Prolong the interaction and maybe even let this person interact with someone else in your presence so you can further observe the shift the person makes in their posture, body language, and even emotional expression. The more time you can give yourself to observe them, the easier it becomes to read into what that person really wants.

#5 Pinpoint action words

Many experts claim that you can easily understand what the other person is thinking and feeling through words even if they won't articulate it. Words represent thought and contained within that is the meaning that you need to know. For example, if your boss says, "I decided to go with brand X," the action word here is decided. From that statement, you can understand a couple of things. First, your boss isn't impulsive. He likes to think things through and prefers to have several options to pick from. What does that mean for you in terms of communicating? Well, if you want him to take action on something you care about, create that same environment where he can "decide." Make a case for your thing and be sure to give him options. It also implies that communicating with him about a decision already made should be thoughtful. It must acknowledge that he is a good decision maker because, based on his words, he views himself that way.

That is something very few people understand when trying to communicate with others. For example, I recently got a random call from my phone company. The woman on the other end of the line was trying to sell me their new WIFI package. Instead of starting the conversation by reading and understanding what kind of person I am, she was too busy trying to shove the new offer down my throat. I explicitly told her that I am very happy with my current phone package and that it has been reliable and served me well over the last several years. I guess no one taught her these techniques that I'm sharing here because her response was, "I know you've been happy with that old package, but quite frankly, you're throwing away money. I'm giving you a much better offer that will allow you to spend much less for much more, and all you have to do make a switch which will take you under ten minutes." I immediately hung up the phone. I felt she not only missed understanding me, but she also insulted my intelligence by stating I've been throwing away money all these years. Why not find a new provider then if I am wasting money on this company?

Action words always offer insights into the way a person thinks and what they value. The more you look for those action words and identify the meaning behind them, the easier it will be to build rapport.

#6 Look for personality clues
Our personalities are as unique as our thumbprints. So, it's up to us as great communicators to become more acutely aware of the traits people around us exhibit. Is someone more introverted or extroverted? Do they seem driven by relationships or significance? What feeds their ego? How does this person behave when stressed? What about when they are relaxed? How closed or open-minded is the person?

By gaining an understanding of one's unique traits, you can more effectively read and, in turn, communicate with them in a way that resonates.

With everything you just learned in this chapter, realize practice makes progress. Learning how to read people accurately will take time, a lot of observation, and the courage to fail. Sometimes you will misread the emotion or intention of another. That's okay. Keep observing, asking questions, and genuinely be interested in the art of communicating effectively.

That's how you enhance all your abilities until you can eventually call yourself a master communicator.

Conclusion

Congratulations! You made it to the end of **Listen with Intention: How to Connect, Create Rapport, Develop Trust and Build Deep Relationships**.

By now, you have the fundamentals of establishing strong two-way communication with anyone on this planet. You've learned strategies, tools, and hacks that can enable you to build rapport and develop trust almost instantaneously. Not only did you learn how to become an active, empathetic listener but also how to show others that you are present. Being able to have a rapport with someone will create mutual respect, attentiveness, and the feeling that you are in sync with another so that you bring about the desired understanding and outcome.

Although becoming a great communicator must begin with you, it's not something you can create on your own. The initial work is self-focused, of course, as you learn to practice mindfulness, control your wandering mind, monitor your body language, and present yourself in the way you would like to be perceived. We talked about the importance of smiling, watching your tone and word choice, as well as body posture, which are all self-focused. But this is only half the equation. The other aspect (equally as important) is practicing empathy and being present with the other person. You need to identify common ground with the other person as early on as possible in your interaction if you're going to build a connection. Find some shared experience, ask open-ended questions, and be genuinely interested in the other person.

Some of the techniques you've learned in this book, such as the Mirror and Match technique, will work wonders as you practice them while engaging in conversation. That means you need to be more aware of the other person's gestures, posture, word choice, and even tone of voice so you can try to match them in a manner that isn't creepy or forced. For example, if the person uses a particular catchphrase several times and you want to make a point resonate, see if you can use the exact words as you convey your message. If the person speaks softly and slowly, then try to lower your volume and pace yourself as you talk. These subtle shifts make the other person feel comfortable. Having said that, let me remind you that many of these skills are tough to master. They require a lot of practice, so start by role-playing with someone who won't get offended if you execute it poorly.

Effective communication and trust-building in our fast-paced, mobile-crazed society can feel overwhelming, especially when most people seem absent-minded. Still, as long as you have the awareness, it is possible to command the listener's attention and make your impact.

Realize that not all communication barriers are due to ignorance. Sometimes the problem is actually scientific. For instance, did you know there's a difference between average speech rate and average processing rate? The average speech rates are between 125 and 175 words a minute. The average processing rate is between 400 and 800 words a minute. So, what does that mean? Many people will want to listen to you, but that "spare time" they get while waiting for you to make your point may lure them into a daydream, causing them to miss a considerable chunk of the message. So before you assume someone is a moron or blockhead, remember there are many reasons why our communication fails.

It is up to us to become more effective so that we can increase the chances of a successful interaction. As you get out there to start practicing everything you've learned, the key takeaway for you is that you need to work on your inner state first. Once you have enough self-awareness, pay attention to what the other person is communicating. Be present and notice their words and their nonverbal cues. Refrain from judgment and use reflective language and open-ended questions to make sure you're both on the same page. In all situations, always strive to come away from that engagement confident that the other person felt heard, understood, and valued. If you can learn to make others feel like you care about them, your message will always land as you intend it.

Good luck!

www.ingramcontent.com/pod-product-compliance
Lightning Source LLC
Chambersburg PA
CBHW071455070526
44578CB00001B/348